the michael jacksons

the michael jacksons

AN ETHNOGRAPHIC MONOGRAPH BY LORENA TURNER

LITTLE MOTH

To My Dear Asher

CONTENTS

ACKNOWLEDGEMENTS

n June of this year, we will mark the fifth anniversary of the untimely death of Michael Jackson. The time has passed quickly. American pop music has adopted new entertainers to hold at its center—Lady Gaga, Justin Timberlake, Katy Perry, Rihanna, Beyoncé—but even in his absence Michael Jackson has never been too far out of that spotlight. Almost weekly there are stories that remind us that there was a Michael Jackson, and that his name, image and everything he touched still has great cultural and economic significance. In fact, just this week, late January of 2014, Justin Bieber was arrested for drag racing and substance use in Miami. Upon his release he posted a picture on Instagram taken after his arraignment along side a similar one of Michael Jackson in 2003, with the caption, "What more can they say" [sic], with an emoji of a crown. This action is a way of paralleling both his arrest experience to Jackson's and as well as the position he feels he inhabits in the pop music landscape. Lady Gaga, too, wants to possess something of Jackson in a public way. It has been reported this month as well, that she wants to buy a share in restoring Jackson's Neverland Ranch in Santa Barbara; this, after purchasing 55 personal items from Jackson's estate in late 2012.

It seems as if Michael Jackson is still the gold standard to which today's pop music stars want to aspire. No one knows this better than the people who work as Michael Jackson impersonators, tribute artists and lookalikes. From the streets of Los Angeles and New York City, in birthday parties, event rooms, and stages both large and small around the United States, these are the people who are on the front line of the collective affections that America has for Michael Jackson. I have spent most of the last five years meeting, befriending, photographing, and listening to these people all over the country. I have seen them perform for small intimate audiences, to large, packed to capacity venues. And in both cases, or in *every* case, the response to their work was both emotional and inspiring. There is no shortage of appreciation for Michael Jackson's work, as there is no shortage of those who want to be connected with him.

"The Michael Jacksons" began one hot summer afternoon in Harlem shortly after Michael Jackson died, when I witnessed throngs of people bouncing up and down, laughing and crying to his music in front of the Apollo Theater. Days later, impersonators roamed the street in front of the Apollo and were mobbed by people there to attend the New York City memorial. I saw a similar scene on Hollywood Boulevard the following week. These moments, these scenes—along with the multitude of representations offered by the impersonators and tribute artists—were in part, the reason I started this project.

This book and project would not have been possible without the support, advice and (sometimes) prodding of many people in my life. Thank you to Jenny Walters and Suzanne Khazaal who made the photo shoots with Dev as MJ and Omar Rajpute incredibly successful. Thank you to Terry Williams at the New School for Social Research for his help to shape the project's essential research questions, and to Helena Holgersson, Rupi Kay, Chris Reiter, Bill Donnelly, Joanna Lehan, and Jean Dykstra for their input and feedback in developing the text. Thank you to Yalithza Noriega for the countless hours she spent with my small son so that I could have open and unfettered time photographing at my studio in Los Angeles in the early, formative stages of the project. Thank you to Meg Handler for the help winnowing down what, sometimes, were 300 pictures from a shoot to a more manageable number, as well as the frequent and enthusiastic conversations about the quality of the work. Thank you to Karen Hu, my assistant in the summer of 2013, for diligently going over every image file and making sure they were perfect.

Thank you, too, to everyone who backed the Kickstarter campaign in 2012 that helped to fund photographing impersonators and tributes in Nevada, Arizona, Texas, Georgia, Florida, Mississippi and South Carolina—Sunny Bates, Kathleen Sharkey, Frank Cefalo, Matt Heltsley, Tomasz Werner, Peter Chiu, Jade Doskow, Terri Warpinski, Steven Hudosh, Lisa Feldstein, Jordan Murph, Austin Eustice, Sarah Shirley, Kevin Wilson, Vivian Greene, Allen Chen, Robin Espinola, Kate Djupe, Alex Suvari, Eileen Sharkey Rosenfeld, Sarita Ekya, and, my friend, John Ensink in the Netherlands.

Thank you to my husband, Peter Sasowsky, for being not just a supporter, but a believer in this project, *and* for being on the receiving end of many conversations that

I needed to have as I made my way from photographer to ethnographer and back again.

The most important thanks and gratitude goes to each and every impersonator, tribute artist and lookalike I met on the road to producing this project. Thank you for graciously letting me into your lives, and, in some cases, your families; thank you for your time, your trust and your friendship. This project exists because every single one of you were generous and kind and welcoming, and it's a privilege to call many of you friends. A million times— thank you.

And, finally, I'd like to single one performer out—Sean Vezina. Had I not met you that sunny February day in 2007 on Hollywood Boulevard, and watched as you danced your heart and soul out on the sidewalk, none of this would have been possible. It is your passion and dedication to your work as a Michael Jackson tribute artist that opened my eyes to the possibility of exploring the nature of the kind of performance documented in this book. Thank you.

LORENA TURNER
Los Angeles, California
January 27, 2014

INTRODUCTION

June 2009, Memorials on the Street, Harlem, New York City

he news first broke on Twitter, "Michael Jackson hospitalized." Within a few hours, on the afternoon of June 25, 2009, it was declared across multiple news outlets that he had died in Los Angeles. Two days later, I heard an impromptu celebration was happening in front of the Apollo Theater, and feeling lucky I was in New York, I headed to Harlem on the number 2 train. The subway ride was crowded, and some riders bore signs of Michael Jackson fandom: buttons, white sequined gloves, and hastily mass-produced bootleg T-shirts memorializing him. When I arrived at the 125th street station, the energy on the street above was palpable. Walking down the sidewalk in that very small section of Harlem, the atmosphere seemed charged, as if prior to a lighting storm. It was late in the afternoon, a light rain shower was tapering off, and sunlight shimmered on the wet streets, splashing a pale orange glow upon the burgeoning crowd there at the corner of Frederick Douglas Boulevard.

As the number of people on the sidewalk swelled, their shouts and cries and comments mingled with the sound of music—Michael's music. The Apollo's red marquee letters read "Michael Jackson—A True Apollo Legend." The doors were locked, the theater remained officially closed, but the sidewalk in front became the epicenter of a kind of semi-spontaneous Michael Jackson memorial. Speakers had been mounted in the doorway, and "Billie Jean," "Smooth Criminal," and "Bad" were on continual rotation. The crowd pulsed with waves of grief and joy along with the music. In between the speakers a small barrier had been appropriated as a makeshift shrine where grieving fans placed flowers, candles, drawings, balloons, notes, and letters—all expressions of gratitude and admiration.

Mourners were instructed to file under the Apollo marquee, leave their offerings, and then move along, but most paused to absorb the moment, and to share in the singing. Some danced despite the crowd's density and lack of space. Some held handmade signs, some had portraits of MJ—photographs and paintings—one middle-aged woman even carried an eighties-era Michael Jackson doll. The crowd bounced and swayed, and sang loudly in unison.

On the fence next to the theater, a large sheet of brown craft paper hung, mourners lifted a rain-smeared clear plastic covering to inscribe their thanks and goodbyes in pencil, crayon, and Sharpie. As the streets dried, I watched a man place a stencil silhouette of Michael Jackson—in the antigravity lean from the "Smooth Criminal" video—to the ground and spray-paint a line of little, white-edged Michaels dancing across the sidewalk. So fulsome was the praise and the reminiscences and celebration that afternoon, that I wouldn't have been surprised if those little Michael silhouettes actually began dancing and singing.

A man holds a painting he made as people gather and sing below the Apollo Theater marquee in commemoration of Michael Jackson's life on the afternoon of June 27, 2009.

The tribute wall next to the Apollo Theater two days after Michael Jackson's death.

I was so intrigued with the size, shape and texture of what I saw that day, that I returned a few days later, on June 30th, when New York City held its official memorial celebration for Michael Jackson. There was no other place it could have been. Michael Jackson's debut NYC performance at the famous Amateur Night at the Apollo on August 13, 1967—with his brothers of the Jackson 5—enthralled the audience, concluded in victory, and directly led to Berry Gordy, a recording contract with Motown, and the release of their first single. Like Amateur Night winners before him—Ella Fitzgerald, Sarah Vaughn, James Brown, Stevie Wonder and Jimi Hendrix—Michael Jackson would forever be associated with the Apollo, at the beginning, and now at the end. Only the Apollo would do for the King of Pop.

hen I arrived, the streets teemed with thousands of people who had arrived hours early for the 2 p.m. memorial, sweating under the hot June sun. Lines snaked around the block along 125th Street, filling the sidewalks six- and seven people deep. The New York Police Department's worn, blue wooden barriers,

A young, unidentified Michael Jackson impersonator performs on 125th Street for people waiting to enter the Michael Jackson memorial event at the Apollo Theater on June 30, 2009.

meant to corral people along the sidewalk and prevent the crowd from spilling into the street, were largely respected, but a handful of MJ tribute artists discovered that the cleared street made an excellent performance space, and jumped the barriers to present their versions of Michael Jackson before a captivated, encouraging audience. These performers represented nearly every transformation in MJ's career. A sharp dressed MJ in tipped fedora and Sgt. Pepper-style military jacket moon-walked near another MJ clad in a sequined vest, with ringlets spilling from under a dark hat, aviator sunglasses concealing the eyes. One striking performer was not more than ten years old. In a white T-shirt, black floodwater pants, white socks, and black shoes, he danced to "Billie Jean." The police turned a blind eye to these transgressions by allowing the performers their space.

Across 125th Street, vendors sold every imaginable form of Michael Jackson memorabilia: concert posters, sparkly fedoras, T-shirts, sequined gloves, buttons. One man laid out a complete collection of Jackson 5 and Michael Jackson albums. Placed on the sidewalk in order of release, the display served as a kind of curated presentation of MJ's forty-year career, from cute, precocious, cherubic, Afro'd, preteen on *Diana Ross*

A retrospective of Michael Jackson's musical accomplishments as an impromptu tribute in Harlem on the afternoon of the Apollo Theater memorial.

Presents the Jackson 5, to the suave, white-suited superstar of *Thriller*, to the metamorphic, lighter skinned, facially altered Michael of *Bad*, *Dangerous*, and *Invincible*. People lingered, conversing with him, reminiscing, and photographing the record covers while he leaned against the wall next to them with the look of a triumphant and true fan on his face.

Along with the street performers, the impromptu sidewalk exhibition seemed to open a new space, within which Michael Jackson might be fully appreciated and celebrated in all his fluid, ambiguous, transgressive, inspiring and fabulously creative identities. And this is what focused my attention.

What occurred in Harlem that afternoon was one of those rare democratic moments—when gender, age, and socioeconomic markers were completely invisible; people self-assembled to celebrate a shared experience, something unique, unscripted and organic. I watched, wandered and photographed for most of the afternoon. My objectives were simple: observe the responses to Michael

The window of the store Pay Half on 125th Street on the afternoon of Harlem's memorial for Michael Jackson.

Jackson's death through the ensuing public reaction, and try and place this into some kind of framework: what does it mean, on an individual level, to lose someone that, for most people, was a symbol without a tangible physical presence? What does the loss of someone like Michael Jackson mean to the culture as a whole? Where did these responses in Harlem—the commercial and personal—the sale of memorabilia, the donning of particular symbolic clothing, the performative display of nostalgia, the creation of graffiti, and the impersonators—come from?

The spirit of what amounted to an extended wake on the streets of Harlem echoed all over the world, as people by the millions mourned the death of an icon, and a man, as widely mocked as he was loved. Years of tabloid scandals—the accusations of pedophilia and sexual abuse, the rumors about failed cosmetic surgeries and the physical transformations, the succession of race defying and gender-bending personas, coupled with the most successful career in popular music history—made "Michael Jackson" synonymous with both "weird" *and* "genius."

The selling of Michael Jackson memorabilia outside the Staples Center while the Los Angeles memorial took place inside on July 7, 2009.

When the Apollo's doors finally opened, admitting groups of 600 people at a time into the theater, the crowds on the streets never seemed to diminish, as every minute more celebrants and mourners poured in from all over the world. Inside, the crowd anticipated a ceremony conducted by Reverend Al Sharpton, as well as musical tributes, and testimonials.

Reverend Sharpton met the moment head-on. "Michael wasn't no freak," he said in front of the crowds still fanning themselves from the heat outside. "Michael was a genius. Michael was an innovator. You can't take someone with extraordinary skills, extraordinary talent, and make him an ordinary person. He was extraordinary. He lived extraordinarily, and we love him with an extraordinary passion."[1]

The outpouring of love *was* extraordinary, and it continued. The following week on July 7th, 31 million Americans—2.5 billion people worldwide—watched the official Michael Jackson memorial, broadcast from the Staples Center in Los Angeles. I stood on the sidewalk outside, just past a line of police officers on bikes, along with other people who didn't win the lottery for a ticket to go inside. We watched a slide show of Michael Jackson's life on a small screen mounted on the side of the building, while inside Stevie Wonder, Magic Johnson, Kobe Bryant, Mariah Carey, Jennifer Hudson, Usher, Brooke Shields, Berry Gordy, and dozens of other music legends, sports figures, and civil rights leaders gathered. Queen Latifah read the poem, "We Had Him," written by Maya Angelou specifically for the event. Nelson Mandela and Diana Ross sent tribute messages from afar.

Writer and musician Greg Tate, captured the source of Michael Jackson's phenomenal global appeal in New York's *Village Voice*.

> From Compton to Harlem, we've witnessed grown men broke-down crying in the 'hood over Michael; some of my most hard-bitten, 24/7 militant Black friends, male and female alike, copped to bawling their eyes out for days after they got the news. It's not hard to understand why: For just about anybody born in Black America after 1958—and this includes kids I'm hearing about who are as young as nine years old right now—Michael came to own a good chunk of our best childhood and adolescent memories. The absolute irony of all the jokes and speculation about Michael trying to turn into a European woman is that after James Brown, his music (and his dancing) represent the epitome—one of the mightiest peaks—of what we call Black Music. Fortunately for us, that suspect skin-lightening disease, bleaching away his Black-ness via physical or psychological means, had no effect on the field-holler screams palpable in his voice, or the electromagnetism fueling his elegant and preternatural sense of rhythm, flexibility, and fluid motion. With just his vocal gifts and his body alone as vehicles, Michael came to rank as one of the great storytellers and soothsayers of the last 100 years.[2]

Tate goes on to celebrate Michael's genius as a popular visual artist, noting how his "phantasmal, shape-shifting videos, upon reflection, were also, strangely enough, his way of socially and politically engaging the worlds of other real Blackfolk from places like South Central L.A., Bahia, East Africa, the prison system, ancient Egypt." And, in a clear and strong response to the much-debated question about Michael Jackson's "blackness," his legitimacy as a black man, Tate directly connected Michael's artistry with "those spiritual tributaries that Langston Hughes described, the ones 'ancient as the world and older than the flow of human blood in human veins.' Bottom line: Anyone whose racial-litmus-test challenge to Michael came with a rhythm-and-blues battle royale event would have gotten their ass royally waxed."[3]

Michael Jackson's death, and the memorials in his honor, all the evocations of all the Michaels around the world, seemed to suspend the racial litmus test. No one remembering Michael in Harlem or L.A. needed one, least of all the impersonators and tribute artists, who not only identify themselves racially along fluid, heterogeneous lines, but very publicly perform transgressive racial and gender identities in defiance of preexisting and restrictive categories. They are men and women, black and white, Asian, Latino, European and African American, and their only litmus test is the response of the audiences for whom they perform the multiple identities of a shape-shifting megastar.

Each chooses from the wide spectrum of possibilities within Michael Jackson's character constructions, mixing dance styles, clothing, and makeup from different eras, and melding these aspects of their performance with changes in Michael's skin color and other physical transformations. Some dark-skinned performers lighten their skin with makeup to achieve their idea of "Michael Jackson," while some light-skinned performers modify and accentuate certain features that help to sell their representation to audiences. An emerging subculture in the world of professional mimicry, these performers represent a much more widespread cultural phenomenon: a sorting-out, and trying-on, and full-bodied acceptance of a profusion of racial and gender identities. I call them "The Michael Jacksons."

I didn't go to the memorials in New York and Los Angeles seeking Michael Jackson mimics, nor did attend because I am a Michael Jackson superfan. I am a photographer and a sociologist, a social scientist with a camera, and I am drawn to big crowds, especially unscripted crowds that come together at a historic moment. I loved the fact that the crowds in Harlem and L.A. gathered spontaneously to honor someone who had been a powerful, soulful force in their lives, and I wanted to photograph those moments and human encounters that expressed the generous spirit of the day. But attending the memorials, I became especially intrigued by the way the impersonators—whom I now call representers—opened a space of pleasure and reflection and possibility. For several years, I'd been watching my photography students, most of whom come from multiple racial and ethnic backgrounds around Los Angeles mimic, appropriate and identify with images and performances of "blackness" in pop culture, and the Michael Jacksons seemed to embody both the fluidity of identity, and the power of blackness as a cultural signifier.

The play and flow of identity enacted by the Michael Jacksons continued to intrigue me in the weeks after the memorials, and I began seeking anyone who claimed to be a professional Michael Jackson performer, starting first in Los Angeles, where many high-profile interpreters live and work. Eventually, I contacted interpreters living and working around New York City, Las Vegas, Texas, Arizona, and several cities across the South.

This book presents the personal and professional lives of a range of performers, from those who work as skilled, highly visible interpreters in New York and L.A., to small-town beginners, dreaming of becoming "authentic" Michael Jackson performers. Among them are Jovan Rameau, a Haitian-born Harvard-educated Michael Jackson look-alike who can make upwards of $500 a day posing for photos with tourists on Hollywood Boulevard, and who longs to be an actor in his own right; Charles "Scooby" James (currently known professionally as MJ.5), an African American college student who performs at birthday parties, in Times Square, and at events in his Queens neighborhood; Jen Amerson, a Caucasian, 37-year-old single mother of two from Florence, South Carolina, who supports her family performing for primarily African American audiences at parties and family reunions in eastern South Carolina; and LaQuinton Holliday, a 16-year-old high school student in Meridian, Mississippi, who envisions impersonating Michael Jackson as a stepping stone toward a performing career very much like the King of Pop's.

For me, performers like them not only dazzled crowds with their dancing and likeness to Michael Jackson, but they also unveiled a moment in which all fixed notions of personal and cultural identity—race, gender, class—were suspended in favor of self-creation and free identity construction.

Ladies and gentlemen. . .the Michael Jacksons.

DEV (Devra Gregory)
Impersonator
San Diego, California
2009

Following spread:
Derrian Tolden
Impersonator
New York, New York
2012

Melissa Weiss and Kevin
Impersonators
Hollywood, California
2009

Jovan Rameau
Impersonator
Hollywood, California
2010

"I left my hometown in Angels Camp, California for an excursion to the top west corner of the country, to Seattle. On the way back, it either rained or snowed on me every day for six weeks and all of my costumes were ruined. I saved up for a new selection of outfits, mainly simple clothes that Michael Jackson would wear on a day off. I looked at thrift stores for these clothes because I knew that I could get quality clothes for a good price and with a name brand label. When I finally got back to Southern California, I had three separate yet complete outfits ready to work in. I made the armband on the maroon satin jacket by individually gluing acrylic rhinestones onto the sleeve. It symbolizes Michael Jackson's love for suffering children throughout the world.

I am dedicated to this. . .I will be different."

Sean Vezina
Tribute Artist
Hollywood, California
2012

Following spread:
MJ.5 (Charles "Scooby" James)
Impersonator
Queens, New York
2010

Bobby Wolfey

"I loved this piece [jacket] when I saw it on Ebay.
It was so different then his other clothes. It stood
out to me. I'd never seen another impersonator
wearing it. The Dangerous Era was also a very
pivotal moment in Michael Jackson's life so
I feel that this is representational of that as well.
It represents to me the strength threw the pain
Michael dealt with at that time. I would wear it to
school, including football games."

Bobby Wolfey
Tribute Artist
Santee, California
2012

Mjx Jackson
Tribute Artist
Matawan, New Jersey
2012

MJ of NOLA (Daron Wilson)
Impersonator
New Orleans, Louisiana
2012

Following spread:
Agent M (Mario Coleman)
Tribute Artist
Houston, Texas
2010

Ian Smith
Tribute Artist
Phoenix, Arizona
2012

Aamir Smith
Impersonator
New York, New York
2010

Jovan Rameau
Impersonator
Hollywood, California
2010

Jovan Rameau
Impersonator
Hollywood, California
2010

Rocky Jackson (Raquel Jean-Joseph)
Tribute Artist
Queens, New York
2011

The Prince of Pop (Omar Rajpute)
Impersonator
Irvine, California
2010

Apple G Jackson (Brandon Hunt)
Impersonator
Las Vegas, Nevada
2012

JenNjuice4MJ (Jen Amerson)
Tribute Artist
Florence, South Carolina
2012

Moonwalker MJ Imitator
Impersonator
Columbia, South Carolina
2012

Scorpio
Tribute Artist
Los Angeles, California
2010

Aamir Smith
Impersonator
New York, New York
2010

63

HollywoodMJ Christof (Christof Ryulin)
Impersonator
Las Vegas, Nevada
2012

LaQuinton

"Impersonating Michael has given me an eye opener
of what he experienced onstage and off. So many
people want to know about you and just talk to you.
Doing this also gives me creative ideas of
performing when it comes to me wanting to be
an entertainer in the near future. People love high
energy, sincere work, and last but not least,
serious commitment & dedication. Michael Jackson's
vision has taught me a lot."

LaQuinton Holliday
Tribute Artist
Meridian, Mississippi
2012

The Prince of Pop (Omar Rajpute)
Impersonator
Irvine, California
2010

Santana Jackson
Tribute Artist
Clearwater, Florida
2012

MJs Raven (Crystal Pullen)
Impersonator
New York City
2012

Domininque Wilson

"'Mikette' came from fellow female MJ impersonator
Moses Harper. She called me that to get my attention
while in a café. My jacket was a plain black jacket that was
designed and arranged by myself. The jacket was free
I added the trimming and style."

Mikette (Dominique Wilson)
Tribute Artist
Newark, New Jersey
2012

Following spread:
Lorenzo Coleman
Tribute Artist
Phoenix, Arizona
2012

Jen Amerson

"I got that jacket from Ebay through a Hong Kong maker. I love it. Its good quality and excellent in lighting. The pants are Docker pants that I have had already, I took them to a professional seamstress and had the red stripe added down the leg. The belt came from a thrift store. The glove from Claire's Boutiques from the mall. T shirt probably through Walmart. My Fedora hat through an online store callled 'Delmonico Hatter.' My leather bracelet reads 'MJ' and that came from an in home selling hostess through a company that sales women's jewelry. My loafers came from an online store called 'Dance store' and my glitter socks came from a friend through facebook that bought them for me through Ebay. It is one of my favorite outfits beside Billie Jean or Dangerous outfit. When I see the pic I smile because it reminds of what I love to do and whom I love which is Michael. I always think to myself, 'Well, this or that could be better and then again I think I am doing alright.' And smile. I have came a long way but I always see room for improvement."

JenNjuice4MJ (Jen Amerson)
Tribute Artist
Florence, South Carolina
2012

Prince Michael Jackson
Impersonator
Atlanta, Georgia
2012

Ray Brooks
Tribute Artist
College Park, Texas
2012

Following spread:
Maxx Vega
Tribute Artist
New York, New York and Newark, New Jersey
2010

J Michael Lucas
Impersonator
Las Vegas, Nevada
2012

CHAPTER ONE

"The pure products of America/go crazy."
A Career Overview

ichael Joseph Jackson was born on August 29, 1958, in Gary, Indiana, an industrial city on the eastern edge of metropolitan Chicago. His mother, Katherine Esther Scruse, a devout Jehovah's Witness from Alabama, dreamt of being a country music star; his father, Joseph Walter "Joe" Jackson, from East Chicago, was a crane operator, a failed boxer, and a onetime guitarist, who, at one time, briefly played in his own R&B band. In 1963, under Joe's guidance, brothers Jackie (whose birth name is Sigmund), Tito (Toriano), Jermaine along with two of their cousins formed a musical group; the following year the two youngest Jacksons—Marlon and Michael, replaced the cousins. They called themselves "The Jackson Brothers".

Gary, Indiana, like much of the industrial Midwest, was near the end of a modest, postwar boom, and set to follow the American steel industry into abysmal decline. The Rust Belt days had arrived. Being performers offered salvation, the promise of money, and a way out, and Joe Jackson, literally and obsessively, drove his children toward stardom. Historian Nelson George notes that in 1966, the Jacksons and the family band, the Jackson 5, began piling into "vans on weekends and holidays to perform. . .building a reputation in black music circles well before signing with Motown."[1]

Like many black entertainers before them, the young Jackson 5 traveled an exhausting interstate tour of African American theaters, nightclubs, and music venues known as "the chitlin' circuit." The circuit clubs were virtually the only places black entertainers could perform in segregated American cities. They ranged from roadside juke joints to legendary venues like the Cotton Club, and featured everything from comedy, to striptease, to the very best rhythm & blues in the world. Performing on the chitlin' circuit, the Jackson 5 followed in the footsteps of Ray Charles, Ella Fitzgerald, Aretha Franklin, John Lee Hooker, Lena Horne, B.B. King, Ike & Tina Turner and dozens of other less heralded, world-class musicians.

But in segregated America, the clubs rarely suited music royalty like those acts. In a 2008 Vanity Fair article, Martha Reeves, lead singer of Martha and the Vandellas, recalled, "We played some horrible places on the chitlin' circuit. We played some places that had horse stables in the back with straw on the floor, places where you had to put fire in the wastebasket to keep warm. At the Apollo Theater, when it was raggedy and dingy and dark before it was renovated, we were in there cooking hot dogs on the light bulbs. We would eat popcorn and sardines, and drink a lot of water to try and feel full."

On the road, and in Gary, the Jacksons lived an intensely musical life. Joe Jackson pushed his sons through grueling rehearsals under the threat of beatings. Katherine led the family in country-western music sing-alongs. The whole family listened to urban blues, soul, gospel, and Motown pop on the radio, and the Jackson 5 played night after night, opening for legends like Etta James, the Temptations, and Jackie Wilson, in Chicago night clubs and chitlin' circuit theaters, studying the scene and absorbing each headliner's moves. Michael was singing along to James Brown on the radio at four years old, and by the time he started performing, at eight, he wrote in his 1988 autobiography, "Moonwalk" he believed he knew Brown's "every step, every grunt, every spin and every turn."[2]

Meanwhile, Gary, a U.S. Steel company town, didn't offer much respite from the road; in many ways it was as oppressive and segregated as any city in the South. The city's steel mills still imposed quotas, limiting how many black workers might advance into skilled trades, and Joe Jackson's crane-operator income afforded the Jackson's only a three-room house. But times were changing. In 1967, Gary elected the nation's first big-city African American mayor, Richard Gordon Hatcher. A committed civil rights advocate, Hatcher identified with the aspirations of the nascent black power movement, delivered speeches with Martin Luther King, and pushed for fair housing and affirmative action, thrilling his black constituents, but sparking secession movements in some of Gary's predominantly white neighborhoods.

Hatcher had spent time with King in nearby Chicago, in 1966, when King and his staff moved there to campaign against housing discrimination and carry the civil rights movement to the North. They were poorly received: Mayor Richard Daley was hostile, civil rights activists were routinely harassed and pelted with bottles, and King himself was hit by a brick. In New York the following year, on April 4, 1967, one year to the day before he was assassinated, King drew even more intense ire when he spoke out against the Vietnam War, calling the United States government "the greatest purveyor of violence in the world today" and strongly linking the war effort to racism. "We were taking the black young men who had been crippled by our society and sending them eight thousand miles away to guarantee liberties in Southeast Asia, which they had not found in southwest Georgia and East Harlem," he said.[3]

At this height of the civil rights movement, the Jacksons drove to Harlem, and on the strength of nine-year-old Michael's breakthrough performance, won the popular Amateur Night competition at the Apollo Theater. Singer-songwriter Gladys Knight witnessed the thrilling performance and recommended the Jacksons to her producer, Berry Gordy, the founder and president of Motown Records. At the time, Gordy passed, reluctant to take on another young act—he was working with seventeen-year-old Stevie Wonder at the time—but the Jackson 5 stayed in the game, and their undeniable appeal left an indelible mark. Within a year Gordy offered them a Motown audition and afterwards promptly signed them to his label.

otown in the 1960s functioned as more than just a record company, it churned at the center of a cultural vortex. When many black artists had little or no professional or artistic freedom, Gordy, a Detroit songwriter and automobile assembly line worker, turned an $800 investment into a wildly successful, culture-changing platform for African American musicians. He did so brilliantly, systematically, and cannily, creating a distinctive sound—Gordy called it "the sound of young America"—that bridged the divide between "black music" and "white music," riding the gathering wave of '60s pop radio into millions of homes across America.

Gordy successfully showcased African American singers, presenting a highly polished, nonthreatening ideal of black pride, achievement, and musicianship. He left nothing to chance; Motown *groomed* its stars. Staff songwriters Smokey Robinson and Barrett Strong, producers Brian and Eddie Holland, renowned etiquette and performing instructor Maxine Powell, and vaudeville performer and choreographer Charles Atkinson, all helped prepare Motown singers for superstardom. They produced a winning formula. Gordy demanded "only hits; no flops" and his team delivered; Motown ruled the charts during the 1960s and '70s, and members of the Motown "family" became household names: the Miracles, the Supremes, the Four Tops, Martha and the Vandellas, Stevie Wonder, Marvin Gaye, Gladys

Knight and the Pips, the Isley Brothers, and, of course, the Jackson 5, brought black music to young America.

Though Gordy didn't promote Motown as a force of social change, and Motown songs were not explicitly *about* inequality or racial justice, the label and its artists were often strongly associated with the civil rights movement and have been widely credited with hastening the end of segregation and ushering African American culture into mainstream American life.

In addition to appealing to a wide, multiracial audience, Motown represented the fulfillment of American aspiration, and the rewards of accomplishment. Motown artists enjoyed wide critical acclaim and enormous commercial success. None of this was destined, and none of it was simple; Motown's existence depended on a constant negotiation with the white-dominated music industry. "In the creative world there were a lot of [black] singers. There weren't a lot of black owners," Motown artist Lionel Richie recalled in an interview from the early 1990s. "[Berry Gordy] *owned* the company. Imagine, this is not happening in the '90s. This is happening during the civil rights movement, during the 1960s—not exactly the greatest land of opportunity for a black businessman. To be a [black] businessman in America then, here's political correctness: 'Yes, sir, no sir. Yes ma'am, no ma'am.' So here's somebody who's somebody saying, 'Go to hell.' This man took no shit."[4]

While taking no shit, Gordy had to work closely with white-owned distribution companies and sell Motown records within the constraints of the white marketplace. "At Motown," he said, "I hired a white salesperson to go to the South. I didn't have pictures of black artists on the record covers until they became big hits. The Isleys had a cover with two white people on the cover. Smokey's 'Mickey's Monkey' had a monkey on the cover. No one knew or cared; they thought it was brilliant."[5]

Motown musicians earned their stature the hard way, often performing on hostile ground. Touring Alabama, Martha Reeves recalled when a shotgun was shoved in her face when the Motown bus stopped at a gas station.

> One of the guys said, "I'm Bobby Rogers of the Miracles. Don't you know about the Miracles?" And he says, "Get back on that bus." He called the sheriff, says, "These niggers are trying to take over my filling station." He didn't know we were down there to make music, not war. He thought, because there's a bunch of black people on the bus, we were Freedom Riders.[6]

In a way, they were. Martha Reeves never sang about civil rights, but as she said, "We were always political. We sold love in front of segregated audiences. That's political."[7] And she also sang "Dancing in the Street," which some heard as a party song, and others heard as a call to arms for social change. During the summer of 1964, "Are you ready for a brand new beat?" could mean many things—and it still carries cultural weight. At a 2011 celebration for Motown at the White House, Barak Obama called "Dancing in the Street", "the soundtrack of the civil rights era."

Julian Bond, former chairman of the NAACP, credits Motown for its singular role in the civil rights movement and American history. "Motown shaped the culture and did all the things that made the 1960s what they were. So if you don't understand Motown and the influence it had on a generation of black, and white, young people, then you can't understand the United States; you can't understand America."[8]

The Jackson 5 joined the Motown family in 1969, moving to Los Angeles to work with Berry Gordy and Diana Ross. Gordy predicted the group would earn three number one records in a row, and they earned four: "I Want You Back," "ABC," "The Love You Save," and "I'll Be There," all topped the charts in 1970. A Motown executive called the Jacksons "the black Beatles." Gordy dubbed their sound "bubble gum soul," and sold their records like candy, by the millions. The Jacksons minted crossover gold. It was a phenomenal start, but the Jackson 5's well-crafted hits didn't necessarily suggest Michael's greatness—until you saw him perform, until you saw him dance.

In 1969, before the wide release of their first hit singles, the Jackson 5 taped their first television appearance, performing the well-known Isley Brothers' song "It's Your Thing" at the newly founded Miss Black America pageant. Moving with ease across the stage like his idol, James Brown, Michael ventured into the audience, following his own groove, while his brothers played their instruments and performed a synchronized dance. While eleven-year-old Michael mesmerized the crowd with his smooth steps and spins, his older brothers looked very much like his backup singers. And that would always be so. Within most of the Jackson 5's carefully choreographed performances, Michael's splendid moves shifted attention away from the group and onto his own unique, magnetic presence. Dominated by his family offstage, onstage, Michael intuitively created a persona and physical presence, which exuded a charisma beyond his years. His voice, too, "worked beyond conventional notions of male soul vocals—even worked beyond gender," notes musician and cultural critic Jason King. "It is not an exaggeration to say that he was the most advanced popular singer of his age in the history of recorded music. His untrained tenor was uncanny. By all rights, he shouldn't have had as much vocal authority as he did at such a young age."[9]

Led by the preternaturally talented Michael, the Jackson 5 performed on a wide range of TV variety shows, like *The Sonny and Cher Comedy Hour* and *The Tonight Show,* which regularly beamed them into millions of American homes. Motown also lent the Jackson 5 name and image to products that appealed to their young fan base: posters, coloring books, lunch boxes, clothes, and a Saturday morning cartoon series on ABC, which debuted in 1971, and eventually ran for two seasons. Scripps College American Studies professor Mathew Delmont describes the series, "The cartoon made the animated image of Michael Jackson and his brothers an important part of the way young people interacted with, or consumed, the groups' music. The Jackson 5 were not just popular, they emerged as extremely visible black presence in an overwhelmingly white medium."[10]

In the cartoon, the Jacksons sported Afros and black leather jackets. When Berry Gordy and Michael were asked by a reporter if the look signaled an endorsement of black power ideologies, a Motown representative stepped in and remarked, "We don't think about that stuff because we were a 'commercial product'."[11] But, of course, because the band *was* a commercial product, millions of Americans got to think about *that stuff* and come to their own conclusions about the meaning of the Jacksons' hair and clothing and demeanor.

By the mid-1970s, Motown's image making had transformed the Jackson 5 into the "The First Family of Post-Civil Rights Young Black America," as drummer, and record producer Questlove described the Jacksons mid-'70s image. "Here," he said, "is a very black, beautiful, proud family with a lead singer well beyond his age in wisdom and performance."[12] This era fostered the album *Destiny,* in 1978 as the Jacksons assumed full creative control over their music. The record's first single, "Shake Your Body (Down to the Ground)" was an unorthodox, inspired hit. This moment "breaks them open for adulthood," claims Questlove, releasing them to explore new musical directions and a new brand of stardom.

At the time, Michael didn't feel like an adult or a star. He'd begun his solo career in 1971 with the single "Got To Be There," making him the first Motown artist pursuing dual careers as a solo performer and band member. His debut album sold more than 1.6 million copies, with "Got To Be There" topping the charts in the United States, Canada, and the UK.

Three more successful solo albums followed between 1972 and 1975. But as the Jacksons rose to "First Family of Young Black America" status, Michael suffered through a painful adolescence.

> It was tough. Everyone called me cute for a long time, but along with all the other changes, my skin broke out in a terrible case of acne. . .I became subconsciously scarred by this experience with my skin. . .My appearance began to depress me. . .The effect on me was so bad that it messed up my whole personality. . .I still had our hit records to be proud of, and once I hit the stage, I didn't think about anything else. . .But once I came offstage, there was that mirror to face again.[13]

He also struggled with the crippling effects of early childhood trauma. Joe Jackson meted out fierce physical punishments to all the members of the Jackson 5, even the youngest. On the road he was also exposed to adult sexuality at an inappropriate age, with his brothers and even more troubling, his father took advantage of the Jackson 5's fame to engage with groupies, sometimes in the same room with Michael.

Much of his youth was a public event, and much a private hell. Clearly young Michael's wounded self-image and his outward success formed fractures in his psyche, creating certain dissonances that fueled his further rise as a pop superstar while nurturing eccentricities that would be praised and criticized with almost equal fervor.

Swimming against those dark undercurrents, Michael Jackson produced his finest work, the solo albums *Off the Wall* (1979) and *Thriller* (1982), two of the most admired and successful records in pop music history. *Thriller* was more than a hit record; it was a worldwide cultural phenomenon. The album was an immediate sensation, leaping up the charts, achieving international acclaim, and earning a record eight Grammy Awards. With an estimated 50-65 million copies sold, *Thriller* remains the best-selling album of all time. In formulating the album's sound—a heady mixture of percolating pop, soul, dance, and rock music—Michael and producer Quincy Jones aimed for a wide crossover audience that the *New York Times* lauded for breaking "the destructive barriers that spring up regularly between white and black music."[14] The *Thriller* videos—especially "Thriller," "Billie Jean" and "Beat It"—elevated music video into the realm of art form and created a new televisual platform for performance and social commentary.

While making *Thriller*, Michael wrote:

> I was determined to present this music as visually as possible. At the time I would look at what people were doing with video, and I couldn't understand why so much of it seemed so primitive and weak. I saw kids watching and accepting boring videos because they had no alternatives. My goal is to do the best I can in every area, so why work hard on an album and then produce a terrible video? I wanted something that would glue you to the set, something you'd want to watch over and over. . .. So I wanted to be a pioneer in this relatively new medium and make the best short music movies we could make. I don't even like to call them videos. On the set I explained that we were doing a film, and that was how I approached it.[15]

The cultural critic Michael Eric Dyson regards Michael's "revolutionary use of the music video" as a vehicle and a visual language that conveys spiritual themes, including "the nature of good and evil; the potentialities for transformation of the self, human nature, and society; the nature of real manhood in American culture; the politics of racial identity in America; and the place of love in changing the world; and a surveying of the politics of American racial identity and awareness."[16] Television in the '80s offered unprecedented global reach, providing the perfect medium for Michael's message. The "Thriller" video, featuring uncommonly coherent storytelling, superb choreography, and state-of-the-art special effects, runs fifteen minutes long, and was broadcast on national television several times a day, month after month in late 1983 and early 1984.

Onstage, Michael Jackson made special effects seem superfluous. Nearly 50 million people worldwide witnessed Michael's first "moonwalk" as he sang "Billie Jean" during Motown's anniversary broadcast, "Motown 25," on May 16, 1983. Questlove recalled the immediate moonwalk craze at his Philadelphia middle school: "The day after 'Motown 25,' by the end of the school day, you saw nothing but black scuff marks crossing the floor from all different directions."[17] Not long after, *Time* reported, "The pulse of America and much of the rest of the world moves irregularly, beating in time to the tough strut of 'Billie Jean', the asphalt aria of 'Beat It.', the supremely cool chills of 'Thriller.'"[18] Michael Eric Dyson later called the "Motown 25" performance an "epochal routine" and celebrated Michael's artistry.

Jackson's uncanny dexterity, disciplined grace, and explosive imagination coalesced in a series of immortal movements, which, in their turn, freeze framed the recrudescent genius of street dance, summarized the important history of Fred Astaire-like purposeful grace in executing dance steps, and extended the brilliant tradition of African American performers like Bojangles, Sammy Davis, and Katherine Dunham surging against the odds to create vital art.[19]

Michael Jackson followed *Thriller* with *Bad* (1987) and *Dangerous* (1991), albums that some critics commended for being more musically accomplished than *Thriller*. Both sold extraordinarily well in their own right. *Bad*, the eleventh best-selling album of all time, sold 30 million copies and had five number one singles, and garnered six Grammy nominations; *Dangerous* sold 20 million and had four top-ten singles. The body of work, and popular reception was unprecedented. "He wasn't just content to make a pop record or a dance record," writes music critic J. Edward Keyes. "Instead, he wanted everything, combining rock guitar with R&B rhythms, disco strings, and the funk of 40,000 years. The production of "Wanna Be Startin' Something" is still baffling and magnificent, fusing a stuttering R&B bass line with traditional African call-and-response chants. Who was doing that then? Who has thought to do it since?"[20]

While the music spoke eloquently for itself, Michael's televisual and sartorial presence also made him a fashion idol. Like many contemporary musical performers, he frequently reinvented himself, refining his dress and appearance and forging fresh looks and identities for each new project, and he did so with an absolute commitment to each new persona and style. He became the ultimate Method actor; he owned and fully inhabited each identity and costume, making pop-culture icons of everything he chose to wear: the wing-shouldered, red leather "Thriller" jacket; the black sequined "Billie Jean" jacket; the white V-neck T-shirt and oversized white dress shirt in which he performed "Man in the Mirror"; the classic "Smooth Criminal" suit and spats; the pegged pants, ankle socks and loafers; the black fedora and crystal-studded glove. Later in his career, onstage and off, Michael came to favor extravagant military-inspired costumes. He often adorned these performance outfits with arrays of zippers, buckles, metal plates or straitjacket-like belts and fasteners. Offstage, he became known during this time as "the King of Pop" with his sharp-shouldered jackets and epaulets, sashes, and gold braids carried the royal military look to its apotheosis. Michael offered his imitators plenty of materials to choose from. For him, though, reinvention came to involve far more than just fashion. His relentless quest to redefine himself, artistically and personally, highlighted an attempt to create a personal narrative—a life, which transcended all conventional and traditional barriers: race, gender, class, generation, and religion.

Rolling Stone, taking account of Michael's career, noted his transcendent cultural impact, as well as his inevitable fall.

> No single artist—indeed, no movement or force—has eclipsed what Michael Jackson accomplished in the first years of his adult solo career. Jackson changed the balance in the pop world in a way that nobody has since. He forced rock & roll and the mainstream press to acknowledge that the biggest pop star in the world could be young and black, and in doing so he broke down more barriers than anybody. But he is also among the best proofs in living memory of poet William Carlos Williams' famous verse: 'The pure products of America/go crazy."[21]

ichael Jackson was surely a pure product of America, and as his fame grew his eccentricities and physical transformations became as starkly evident as his genius. The slight frame, thin voice, and childlike speech contrasted sharply with the fierce energy that commanded the stage and enthralled his audience. He rode the wave of his fame until it crested in 1993, the year he performed during the Super Bowl XXVII halftime show. It was also the year he was accused, for the first time, of child sexual abuse. Only two more studio albums were released in his lifetime, *HIStory: Past, Present and Future, Book I* in 1995, and *Invincible* in 2001.

All the while, Michael withdrew deeper into a world separate from his public image. His changing facial structure, skin color, and hairstyles prompted endless speculation about his racial identification, sexual orientation, and even his gender identification. He became a constant target and an easy punchline for late-night talk show comedians. While he had been the butt of many jokes since the '80s, now the jokes and observations grew meaner, less amused, and more accusatory. In their article, *Michael Jackson, Television and Post-Op Disasters*, the sociologists Macarena Gomez-Barris and Herman Gray chronicle his physical and behavioral metamorphosis. They describe him from moving from "cute, young, Black singer" to possessing "weird, unfixed racial identity in his adult years".

Michael was fiercely criticized for bleaching his skin, though according to his dermatologist, Dr. Arnie Klein, he suffered from Vitiligo, an autoimmune disorder that compromises the body's ability to produce melanin, or skin pigmentation. Regardless, his pale skin, paired with the modifications made to his face—slimming the nose, sharpening the jawline, and making his cheeks more pronounced—created a hybrid racial and gender identity, which was, and is, liberating to some, deeply troubling to others. His use of makeup, too, to emphasize the roundness of his eyes, the deep arch of his eyebrows, the evenness of his skin tone and redness of his lips, also clashed with cultural ideals of blackness and masculinity.

Though Michael was married and divorced twice (the first time to Elvis Presley's daughter, Lisa Marie), he was infrequently publically linked with any romantic partners. He was, however, the father of three children—Prince Michael was born in 1997, Paris in 1998, and Prince Michael II ("Blanket") in 2002, whom, after a brief marriage to the biological mother of the first two, he raised as a single parent. His youngest child was born via surrogate. Accusations of child molestation and abuse in the 1990s and early 2000s, coupled with reports of his childlike life at his Neverland Ranch outside of Santa Barbara, California—which included an amusement park—further complicated the public perception of the "real" Michael. Was he gay? Was he straight? Was he a man-child? Was he still black? Did he really want to be white?

In media appearances and interviews, of which there are only eighteen in both print and broadcast outlets during his career, he addressed many of these questions obliquely. For example, in a 1995 interview with Diane Sawyer on *Prime Time Live*, he and his then-wife, Lisa Marie Presley, were asked, "What is a 36-year-old man doing sleeping with a 12-year-old boy, or a series of them?" His response: "I have never invited anyone into my bed, ever. Children love me, I love them. They follow me; they want to be with me. But...anybody can come in my bed, a child can come in my bed if they want."[22]

The question of who Michael Jackson was may go unanswered for some, but for many the question has become a subject of their subjective interpretation. As for The Michael Jacksons, theirs are performances of a polymorphous self-creation, which defy received notions of gender, sexuality, age, and race. And this liberating force appears to have intensified, now that he's gone. Unfettered by his tragic personal history, by any character flaws, by the feeble constraints of a body, Michael Jackson, the idea, perseveres.

When Michael Jackson died, the world's critical gaze softened for a time, and his popularity and influence surged anew. Between June 2009 and June 2010 his estate earned roughly $1 billion. A movie compiled from rehearsal footage documenting his final days has become the highest grossing performance film ever. In the winter and spring of 2012, Cirque du Soleil developed a touring acrobatic show, "Michael Jackson: the Immortal World Tour," which played to sold-out crowds in cities across the United States.

In song, dance, and fashion, Michael Jackson remains a formidable presence. Usher, Rihanna, Chris Brown, Justin Bieber, Bruno Mars, all clearly owe Michael a great debt. Justin Timberlake channels Michael's moves in the 2013 music video "Suit & Tie" and Beyoncé sports a single, metal Cyborg glove in "Single Ladies." From Jay Z, to Kanye, to Coldplay, current pop stars don tilted fedoras and MJ-style military jackets. And legendary rapper and record producer Timbaland, who has worked with Justin Timberlake, Jay Z, and Robin Thicke, is, in August of 2013, rumored to be producing a new posthumous Michael Jackson album, blending his own distinctive sound with MJ's vocals.

In the wider world, Michael Jackson, and what he represents to new generations continues to evolve and grow in complexity, and paradoxically, in simplicity. The once unavoidable interrogations about race, gender, and sexuality may seem irrelevant, if not quaint, to young people. To those who only knew the post-'90s Michael Jackson, he simply was what he was—Michael—a person, a performer, and to some, an inspiration.

On the streets, in tribute performances from New York to Los Angeles, to senior center recreation rooms, to private birthday parties, performers, men, women children—of the multitude of ethnicities—present individualized representations of this cultural force. In short, Michael Jackson simply multiplied after June 2009 into the Michael Jacksons.

CHAPTER TWO

"The all-American fascination with Blackness."
The Performance of Race, A Brief History

he Michael Jacksons represent something unique that once seemed audacious—a cross-cultural performance that adapts physical aspects race into the performer's craft, costume, makeup and gestures. The performers walk a line, aware of the sad, fraught history of race and stereotype and mockery, but somehow unselfconscious about their own motives and presentation.

White entertainers' imitations of black artists—from mimicry to appropriation to sincere homage—have long been a disquieting current in American popular culture, springing from what Greg Tate calls "the all-American fascination with Blackness." The peculiar desire in white America to sample, appropriate, and scrutinize black culture that emerged in minstrelsy, evolved into a voracious national appetite for African American creativity.[1] Originating informally in the social arrangements of slavery, the appropriation urge ultimately became an organized, market-driven force, peaking in the twentieth century when "much of what America sold to the world as uniquely American in character in terms of music, dance, fashion, humor, spirituality, grassroots politics, slang, literature, and sports was uniquely African American in origin, conception, and inspiration," says Tate. Rarely, however, did racial fascination recognize the genius and subjectivity of actual African Americans, nor the black foundations and influence of much American art and music. Fusing desires for imitation and segregation, pleasure and erasure, minstrelsy became a definitive racial meme, absorbing signifiers of blackness while transmitting the many dehumanizing mythologies and stereotypes that continue to haunt American culture.

s early as the seventeenth century, the white musicians of North America freely borrowed from African American music, and by the beginning of the American Revolution, white entertainers ritually imitated black musicians for white audiences. In 1830s, what began as a confluence of musical currents had become a strange, enormously popular form of race-based entertainment: the minstrel show. In minstrel shows, white performers masqueraded as stock slave characters. They painted their faces black with burnt cork or greasepaint, dressed in ridiculous costumes, and crudely mimicked African American forms of song and dance. From the blackface characters of the minstrel shows come crippling, long-lived stereotypes: Jim Crow, the carefree slave; Mr. Tambo, the cheerful musician; and Zip Coon, an ostentatious free black man who did not "know his place." The characters were mercilessly mocked, however many minstrels were talented musicians. Their repertoire constituted the first authentic American music; songs like "Camptown Races" and "Swanee River", and most of the songbook of Stephen Foster.

After the Civil War, African American performers adopted the blackface mask; imitating white artists who were themselves imitating black people for entertainment. It was the only way black musicians could earn a living; they were otherwise prohibited from publicly performing for pay. Behind the mask of their white artist counterparts, African American musicians found a measure of cultural mobility while subtly subverting minstrel stereotypes. By the 1890s, black composers and performers were breaking into the entertainment business through the minstrel show.

Still, it was a white-dominated business and blackface performances continued well into the twentieth century, notably in Hollywood movies starring prominent white entertainers, such as *The Jazz Singer* and the films of Judy Garland, Mickey Rooney, and Bing Crosby. Black actors, too, emerged from the minstrel show. Lincoln Perry's work in popular Hollywood films of the 1920s and '30s represented minstrelsy's stereotypes. Known by the stage name Stepin Fetchit, Perry's screen persona was a seemingly lazy, slow-talking, urban-dandy servant, a version of the Zip Coon character called "subversive" for his unwillingness to serve at the pleasure of white people. Bert Williams performed the Mr. Tambo character in blackface on Broadway in the Ziegfeld Follies for eight years.[2] Bill Robinson's Bojangles was an elegant tap dancer, actor, and frequent Shirley Temple sidekick who directly influenced Fred Astaire: the latter's blackface tap routine called "Bojangles of Harlem" in the film *Swing Time* was an overt tribute to Robinson.[3]

Astaire's blackface performance is a strange form of homage, but not a culturally empty one, and certainly not merely an exploitive one. As filmmaker and cultural theorist Manthia Diawara writes, stereotypes always "rob people of their history and shun their realism," but performance can turn a rigid stereotype into something more fluid and complex, an artistic expression that gives dimension to a caricature, disrupts convention, or opens up a cultural space. Bert Williams' Bojangles was based on a minstrel type, but his performance gave the character a measure of subjectivity, and created a public, theatrical presence for the next generation of black entertainers, who broke away from imposed representations of race and created their own. Fred Astaire, it appears, used the recognizable blackface type to acknowledge and celebrate Williams' influence on American dance. As a form of popular entertainment, mimicking race—white performers playing black characters; black entertainers becoming white performers pretending to be black—suggested that racial identity was fluid, rather than fixed. Indeed, cultural studies scholar J. Martin Favor maintains that, ultimately, "race" is socially constructed and performable, if not always performed, "Race is theatrical—it is an outward spectacle—rather than being anything internal or essential."[4]

And the performance of race depends upon a series of exchanges. While white blackface performers often played on degrading African American culture, they also revealed a desire and admiration for black culture—at least in the liberated moment of play. At the same time, the degraded culture of black America had been taught to aspire to white ideals of beauty, culture and sophistication. It barely needs mentioning that African American culture became thoroughly psychologically colonized by the dominant culture's ideals and aspirations. The drive to achieve notions of physical likeness to Caucasian features, created an industry worth millions of dollars in hair-straightening products, hair dyes, skin-lightening cosmetics and the like. In his autobiography, Malcolm X recounted the pain he endured in the "conking" process, a brutal chemical system that employs lye to straighten the kink out of hair to achieve a "white" look. Even all these years after the black power movement—summed up in the slogan, "black is beautiful" and the rejection of such methods to attain "white" appearances—the products and styles continue and evolve; hair extensions, wigs, and skin-lightening products inhabit large portions of beauty aisles in neighborhoods across the country. While the '60s civil rights movement, and more radical leaders like Malcolm X, rejected of the white ideal, and called into question the psychological and sociological pathologies these processes exposed, the products and styles persist, for better or worse. This interchange continues to flow between black and white cultures, with certain points of contact tending toward a common mean, a blurring of origins, and an integration of cultures.

However, power, and "race," as it has been defined in America, meant rigid segregation also, and the systematic denial of human, constitutional, and economic rights to generations of African Americans, a stark reality that continues to define the cultural space where black artists live and perform. Peculiarly American conceptions of race—the fascination with blackness and its marketability, paired with pathologically distorted mythologies about black culture—profoundly shaped the modern music business, which was as segregated as every other American institution, and actively sought out, and promoted, white artists who could impersonate the sounds of pioneering black musicians. Inevitably, appropriation marginalized African Americans and African American music.

But if segregation meant that white audiences discovered black music through Benny Goodman, Elvis Presley, and the Rolling Stones, twentieth century mass media, particularly radio, allowed *anyone* to listen to Duke Ellington, Chuck Berry, Aretha Franklin, and Otis Redding—and hear the deep, black roots of American music. Against the grain of segregation, the collective experience of popular music in the mid-twentieth century disarmed racial stereotypes and created a fledgling cultural space in which new, self-determined expressions of identity, love and fellowship could be performed. Michael Jackson inherited that space, lived there with verve and heart, and invited the world to live there with him.

Michael Eric Dyson places Michael among the company of Charlie Parker, Wynton Marsalis, Romare Bearden, and Betye Saar, artists "who have wrestled existentially and artistically with disenabling forms of otherness and difference," artists who offer "crucial resources for contesting the disempowerment that can result from political, economic, social and cultural marginality."[5]

Michael did so by striking "a deep, primal chord in the human psyche, fascinating us, perhaps, because he so easily and eerily represents us, even mirrors us (all of us) at the same time. Thus, if he is not a Nietzchean *Ubermensch*, he is a Promethean allperson who traverses traditional boundaries that separate, categorize, and define difference: innocent/shrewd, young/old, black/white, male/female, and religious/secular."[6]

And Michael's artistic form, music, always stirs the drink. Perhaps more than any other cultural artifact the collective experience of popular music creates a space in which, says Dyson, "the friction between cultures can be utilized as something that generates a positive force," where black and white creativity might create something new. Crafting a broadly inclusive body of work inspired by West African, African American, and European music as well as the moves and grooves of James Brown, Fred Astaire, and Jerome Robbins. "His racial inbetweeness made him more, and not less of, an essential figure in our tradition," wrote John Jeremiah Sullivan in his 2011 book, *Pulphead: Essays*. Michael Jackson perhaps like no other figure exemplified this rich and troubled confluence of cultures, histories, and exchanges.

The Michael Jacksons live in that hybrid space, too. Representing Michael draws them along into history's wake, and the ongoing deconstruction of received racial identities in favor of polymorphous self-creation. Their performances, the particular ways in which they create the character of Michael Jackson, transcend skin color, racial identity *and* gender identity, delighting and unsettling audiences, and even, at times, challenging their own notions of self. Some representers turn racial imitation on its head, creating moments in which racial and gender categories flow freely and more negotiabley than they may in everyday life. These performances, indulge, explore, and expand the forces and traditions that have played in the fields of American music for hundreds of years.

Most notably, the Michael Jacksons, especially those under thirty years old, are not overly troubled by the details of Michael's personal life. They are far less interested in diagnosing or scrutinizing his private behavior than in celebrating his genius as a performer. They simply read him differently. His skin color does not suggest a failed allegiance to blackness, as it did for many people of earlier generations, and his altered features do not signal self-hatred. In fact, many performers celebrate those transformations in their representations of Michael. They are not race, or gender-obsessed; *their* Michael Jackson is neither black nor white, male nor female, but a hybrid, uniracial person like themselves. The youngest representers, many of whom strongly connect to Michael's compassion and social conscience, tend to see him more as an iconic figure, a prophet, or a saint, or an avatar of loving kindness. Michael's performances told them all they need to know.

Their stance is a refreshing rejoinder to the more widespread urge to pathologize and condemn Michael Jackson. As Sylvia J. Martin notes, "a performance perspective" allows us to "shift our gaze" from Jackson's psyche and motives to his art, to the ways in which his performances contested racial constraints and empowered people to redefine their place in the world. While Michael's skin "engendered suspicion and sensationalism from the media, he also challenged received notions about the commensurability between skin color and racial identity, using his body to destabilize perceptions of essentialism."[7] If his pale skin suggested a kind of race betrayal, performances such as "They Don't Care About Us," a music video shot with Spike Lee in a favela in Sao Paulo, and in Salvador de Bahia,

Brazil, key sites of the nineteenth century slave trade, strongly signified Michael's deep, nuanced connection to his African American identity. Questlove has said that *all* of Michael's moves "flag and signal his African pride."[8]

CHAPTER THREE

"They love Michael."
Hollywood Boulevard

n 1991, Hollywood store clerk Nicole Kim lamented to *Los Angeles Times* reporter Eric Young, "The Boulevard is losing fame. The streets are dirty and crazy people are begging around." During Hollywood's worst down and out years, the theater lights around Hollywood Boulevard and Highland Avenue grew dim and the area's luster tarnished. The Boulevard became synonymous with "sordid" and "shady," if not downright "sleazy." Throughout the 1990s crime was rampant, vagrancy was highly visible, and prostitutes and drug addicts made the streets their haven.

That same year, 1991, an aspiring actor and waiter working at a local restaurant heard yet another customer tell him, "You look a lot like Christopher Reeve." Inspiration struck. With a week's tips, the waiter, Christopher Dennis, bought blue, red and gold material, constructed a costume, and became Hollywood Boulevard's—and the world's—first sidewalk Superman. The response was tremendous, and he began earning more than $600 a day in tips. Within a few years, other entrepreneurial impersonators took to the Hollywood streets to interact with tourists: Spiderman, Batman, Darth Vader, Big Bird, Elvis, Marilyn Monroe, Madonna, Captain Jack Sparrow, and Michael Jackson, figures and figments of popular culture all began appearing daily at the corner of Hollywood and Highland to traverse the brass outlined terrazzo stars of the Walk of Fame. A new space for play and imagination was born—part Hollywood dream and part desperation, part celebrity and part anonymous wannabe.

Over the next decade, the area around Hollywood and Highland underwent a facelift. In 2000, Grauman's Chinese Theater (renamed the TCL Chinese Theaters in 2013), the

historic cornerstone of the block, began a large restoration and modernization project. Originally opened in 1927, with the premiere of Cecil B. DeMille's *King of Kings*, TCL Chinese Theaters experienced several cycles of glamour and neglect, but now once again draws tourists and stargazers from all over the world into its orbit. Close by, in 2001, after an eleven-year renovation, the Walt Disney Company reopened the El Capitan Theater.
The El Capitan, once a lavishly decorated movie house, known as "Hollywood's First Home of Spoken Drama," had languished for years in silence and decrepitude. Under the Disney marquee the theater now features first-run Disney films and high-profile film premieres.
A few months after the El Capitan reopening, the modern Kodak Theater opened. Though the name was changed in 2012 to the Dolby Theater, after Kodak filed for bankruptcy, it plays host to the annual Academy Award ceremony and is considered the crown jewel of the Hollywood & Highland retail complex along side dozens of stores including Forever 21, Victoria's Secret, and American Eagle Outfitters. Jimmy Kimmel tapes his live nightly show, right next to the El Capitan Theater. And steps away, stands the Pantages Theater and the Hollywood Roosevelt Hotel, home to the first Academy Awards ceremony, in 1929, and a recent hot spot for young Hollywood celebrities.

In the middle of this Hollywood renaissance and newly rediscovered glamour, celebrity impersonators work the Walk of Fame, specifically the strip of sidewalk between Highland and Orange Avenue along Hollywood Boulevard. This is where the impersonators and tourists mingle; the tourists stopping to photograph each other over the name plaques commemorating more than 2,400 celebrities, from Paul Anka and the Andrews Sisters to Bruce Willis and Mickey Mouse.

The tourists and the street performers and impersonators engage in an interesting dance on the sidewalk there. The performers await the subtle signals of an interested tourist—the flash of recognition, acknowledgement, eye contact, or perhaps a camera slightly raised. Once the connection has been made, the performer may draw the tourist in with a smile and agree to be photographed—for a few dollars per customer. The street performers are prohibited to officially charge for photos—many of the characters present are owned, or trademarked, by entertainment corporations, and outright payment would constitute commercial use and copyright infringement—so instead the impersonators and street performers request compensation in the form of a "donation" or "tip." To avoid uncompensated photography, the performers employ various tactics, like blocking their own faces with a hand or a fan, or ducking out of the frame. The gesture is firm, but the give and take is easygoing; the impersonators are *working*—they're trying to make a living, after all—

but both performers and tourists willingly and playfully spin pop culture fantasies, and everyone wants the show to go on.

And it does. Any day of the year, anytime of day, Marilyn Monroes and Madonnas and Michaels Jacksons put themselves on display in the two blocks west of Hollywood and Highland. I took my first photographs of a Michael Jackson in February 2007, when I brought my camera to the intersection, drawn by the possibility to photograph the behavioral exchanges between the masses of people and the celebrity impersonators on the Walk of Fame. At an impromptu sidewalk performance there, a crowd had gathered around a young man wearing a blue satin shirt tucked into black jeans cinched with a large black belt. Long tendrils of black curly hair spilled from beneath a tilted fedora. To his right sat a large boom box pumping "Billie Jean." He spun in circles, stopped, and deftly raised his body on the points of worn, black penny loafers, perfectly capturing an iconic Michael Jackson move for the surrounding crowd. When he finished performing a song, he carried around a small, white plastic bucket, into which his audience tossed quarters, dimes, nickels and dollar bills. He nodded his thanks as he weaved through the crowd.

The crowd disbanded and the sidewalk was once again opened up as a thoroughfare. The tourists again perused the stores and stargazed and snapped pictures. The young man then stepped to the side and took his place in a lineup of other ersatz superheroes and celebrities. Some laughed and quietly talked with each other, while a few chatted up passersby. But the young man kept to himself, recovering from his performance.

I approached him and put a few bills into his bucket, telling him he was great.

"The crowd really loved your performance," I said.

"They love Michael," he replied.

Standing close to him, I could see that he did not naturally resemble Michael Jackson at all. He was Caucasian, albeit with a deeply tanned face, and the hair escaping from beneath his hat turned out to be a rather precariously perched wig. Little wisps of his natural light brown hair could be glimpsed around his hairline. Slender, at a height of about 5 feet 7 inches, his clothes billowed around him. He wore silver mirrored sunglasses; the kind police in '70s movies wear.

He told me his name was Sean Vezina. I asked him about his work as a Michael Jackson impersonator, how long he'd been doing it, and if there were others. Still out of breath, beads of sweat rolling down his face and dotting his satin shirt, he answered, "Yes, a few."

He looked around and pointed down the block. A tall man practiced some Michael

Jackson-style dance moves on the sidewalk. His costume consisted of the familiar black pants, a white shirt, and a red vest. The pants rode high on his waist, revealing thin ankles covered with white socks, his feet shod in worn black loafers. He, too, wore a fedora, and a wig, though the hairstyle was shorter than Sean's. He was African American, but wore makeup—a lighter tone than his actual skin. Clearly, he played a different version of Michael Jackson. Michael from the late '90s or early 2000s, the light-skinned Michael Jackson.

Two years passed before I encountered more Michael Jackson impersonators. And on 6 July 6, 2009, the night before the memorial scheduled for Michael Jackson in Los Angeles, I flew into town and drove straight to Hollywood and Highland hoping to find one, and hoping to see an outpouring similar to what happened in Harlem.

CHAPTER FOUR

"I contradict myself; I contain multitudes."
July 2009, The Los Angeles Memorial for Michael Jackson

he night before the Michael Jackson memorial in Los Angeles, the sidewalk at the intersection of Hollywood and Highland felt like the right place to be. As I arrived, two impersonators mimicked and mimed their ways through MJ dance routines for a crowd several hundred strong. Fans wearing "RIP Michael" T-shirts walked and mingled in small groups, and couples took pictures of each other and the impersonators. But no money changed hands. There seemed to be a shared sense that the performances that day served as a form of tribute and memorialization, and the exchange of money would denigrate the memory of Michael Jackson.

Michael's star on the Walk of Fame lay at the hub of the L.A. street memorial. When a Walk of Fame celebrity dies, the Hollywood Chamber of Commerce sets out a thin iron stand upon which a wreath or bouquet of flowers rests. Sometimes the emotion is palpable, and sometimes only the anonymous pathos. The lone stand angled just slightly on the sidewalk, the white flowers and ribbon catching the bright Los Angeles sun and blowing softly in the breeze. As people pass, they may read the name, and try to recall where they've seen or heard it—on TV? In a movie? On the radio?—but on the day before Michael Jackson's memorial, no such questions were asked and nylon barriers appeared around his star. As with the doorstep at the Apollo, it eventually created a deep repository for offerings brought to the site.

When I arrived, the small rectangular space within the barriers overflowed with flowers and notes and miscellaneous offerings. An onlooker there told me that over the past two weeks the star had been cleared three or four times a day to make room for

An unidentified Michael Jackson performer on Hollywood Boulevard the evening before the Los Angeles memorial.

new visitors to place more notes, cards, flowers, and effigies.

Around the star, a crowd gathered several deep, and as they photographed the cards, flowers, posters, photographs, letters, and each other, I photographed them. At one point, a television correspondent appeared with his cameraman. He wanted opinions and insight from people in the crowd: Who was Michael Jackson? What will his loss mean? How will his life best be celebrated? A man walked through the crowd holding up his car's license plate, succinctly expressing his reason for being there—LOVE4MJ. He appeared to be a perfect interview subject and one of the correspondents ran over and pushed a microphone towards him.

A woman dressed in a hot pink satin sleeveless gown and long pink gloves—clearly emulating Marilyn Monroe in the "Diamonds Are a Girl's Best Friend" musical number from *Gentlemen Prefer Blondes*—materialized next to Michael's star. Her ill-fitting dress was wrinkled and stained. The hem was grimy where it swept the sidewalk, and her gloves were frayed.

Michael Jackson's star on Hollywood Boulevard's Walk of Fame on the night of July 6, 2009.

Her thin body bore the freckled and over tanned evidence of years in the Southern California sun. A frizzy, matted platinum-blond wig sagged around her head. As we talked that evening, she seemed completely unaware that these aspects of her appearance revealed the "seams" of her character construct. Her name was Melissa. I met Melissa in 2007 while photographing the crowds who line up to watch celebrities enter the Kodak Theater before the Oscars ceremony. Melissa was very eager that I take her photograph back then, and I consented. Afterwards she seemed very anxious to view the proofs. I emailed her a contact sheet with the request that she choose the ones she wanted. In the end, she was appreciative but extremely critical of the images. I printed her choices and sent them to her, despite her apparent dissatisfaction, then kept in touch with an occasional text message over the following year.

But that night, at Michael Jackson's Hollywood star, she recognized me immediately, even though it had been two years since I had photographed her.

"You're that photographer!" she shouted over the noise of the crowd.

She was escorted by one of the Michael Jackson impersonators I had seen performing earlier that night. She motioned me to follow her and grabbed the man dressed as Michael by the arm. Along the way, he was introduced as Kevin. We crossed Hollywood Boulevard to Jimmy Kimmel's theater and stopped in front of a large plywood wall, a temporary barrier by a storefront undergoing renovation. Glossy black paper hung from its surface. The sun was setting, but just enough light remained to take pictures. Melissa pulled Kevin in front of the black wall and looked at me, "Don't worry, she's a great photographer," she said. I didn't feel like a great photographer, not even close, and after our last photography-related exchange, I would never have expected to hear her make that claim. But sometimes "greatness" in someone's eyes—even if it is mere flattery—creates opportunity. In this case, Melissa's perspective, and Kevin's expectation, had brought me to a moment that proceeded to unfold in ways I hadn't anticipated.

Melissa placed her back against the wall and turned broadly towards me. I raised the camera to my eye and peered through the viewfinder. She quickly affected the air that accompanies overacting, her finger went to her lips and she bit her index finger, her eyes bore a slightly pained expression. I pressed the shutter release. She angled her head slightly. Again I took her picture. She pulled Kevin in close and instructed him on where to put his hand and arm, what to do with his head.

"But Marilyn wasn't around when Michael Jackson was," I said, probing.

"I'm Madonna from the 'Material Girl' video," she retorted. I knew this, but needed to hear it from her to validate what we were doing.

Kevin angled his body into Melissa's, looking forward and holding his head high. I fumbled with the camera snapping about ten shots. Every time I clicked the shutter I moved slightly and refocused the lens. Melissa and Kevin, by then completely enmeshed in their Madonna and Michael Jackson characters, moved slightly after every shot, almost in time with me.

Then, just as quickly as things came together, they unraveled. The evening sunlight started to fade, and Melissa and Kevin's connection to each other—and to their characters—receded.

I told them I was done, that I got what I wanted, though I really had no idea what I was looking for, or what I had captured. I took a few steps back and looked down reviewing the pictures on the back of my digital camera. It was an odd thing. Melissa and Kevin had reenacted a relationship that, in the public eye, existed briefly; the night Michael Jackson

A display of affection on Hollywood Boulevard, July 2009.

and Madonna escorted each other to the Oscars in 1991. But the actual event didn't look anything like their portrayal. Melissa's Madonna came from a 1985 music video, which itself had been mimicry of Marilyn Monroe from 1953. Kevin's portrayal was a stylized version of the 1995 military-style wear Michael favored around the release of *HIStory*, and the loose-fitting, open-to-the-navel white oxford evoked the *Dangerous* era, from around 1991.

In the photograph, Melissa's face expresses a longing to be taken seriously and a desire for her performance as a starlet to be validated. But the lines in her face, and the tone and texture of her skin, pierced the façade she longs to enact. Her back, slightly arched, further emphasizes her dedication to the character. Kevin didn't talk much through the whole experience. When I initially saw him, I had the sense that he was not interested in molding an authentic representation of Michael Jackson—for one thing, he was white, and didn't wear any makeup (not even eyeliner, or a black smudge on the chin to create Michael's cleft). A few of his teeth were missing, or black with rot, and lower part of his face

Kevin and Melissa pose as Michael Jackson and Madonna on Hollywood Boulevard.

appeared sunken; his black wig was matted, like Melissa's and only called attention to its own falseness. His lack of authenticity, in fact, screamed "opportunist," especially in the context of Hollywood Boulevard on the eve of Michael Jackson's memorial. However, he wasn't collecting money, so the motivation for his presence remained unclear. His Michael Jackson presented none of the ambiguity of race or gender or sexuality, none of the lightness and innocence that I'd come to associate with the real performer. His lack of commitment seemed at odds with Melissa's portrayal of Madonna. Yet, for that moment of that one photograph—perhaps it was of the degree of separation between his fingers or the rigidity of his hand as it was placed in front of his hip—he was entirely convincing.

The sidewalk across from Staples Center the next morning was a relatively lifeless scene. Though the giant video screen on the side of the arena flashed a slide show of highlights from Michael Jackson's public life, seemingly an invitation to participate in the memorial, people without tickets were kept far away, held at parking-lot feeder streets by concrete barriers and teams of bicycle-riding police. The message was clear. Before long, vendors outnumbered onlookers and most of the interactions were commercial. Nearly alone in spontaneous mourning and appreciation, Kirby Shields presented a collage of photographs and memorabilia assembled on a three-paneled folding screen, a personal tribute in the spirit of the Michael Jackson album display I'd seen in Harlem two weeks before.

I went back to Hollywood and Highland that afternoon, looking for Sean Vezina, the first Michael Jackson impersonator I spoke with when I originally went to photograph Hollywood Boulevard in 2007. I walked the Boulevard and asked around. I asked other impersonators about him, but no one had seen him. Feeling slightly defeated, I decided to catch the subway home. Suddenly, Sean emerged from the escalator at the darkened entrance to the subway. We greeted each other and began walking together. He looked different, many years older and more gaunt than when I'd last seen him. But he was very much alive, and fully in character in his ambling, approximating way. He wore a woman's short, black velvet blazer, a red satin shirt, jeans, a silver sequined armband on his right arm, mirrored sunglasses, and a perfectly pitched black fedora. He was free of makeup, and, like Kevin the night before, a cheap black wig rested beneath his hat, though he had taken great care to grow and shape his sideburns and color them black. His costume was clearly based on an outfit Michael Jackson wore while performing "Dangerous" for a Democratic Party fundraiser called, "A Night at the Apollo" in 2002.

Sean carried himself with an ease and sense of purpose. He kept his hands folded in front of his body between his waist and chest. Before he arrived that day, he told me, he had decided to take a memorial walk through the neighborhood, in character, interacting with people as Michael might have. He planned to walk east down the boulevard, towards Michael's star, then across Hollywood Boulevard, and down the other side of the street in front of El Capitan, then to the intersection of Highland. Slightly unsure of my place in all of this, and even more uncertain of what role he would play, I wrestled with my camera to capture something of his interactions with "the fans," as he called them. The sun rose high in the Los Angeles sky and his hat cast deep shadows across his face. He told people that I was his photographer, a claim that served to validate both of our appearances that day.

"Michael! Michael!" called people from all directions. He shook hands with everyone who came forward and posed for pictures with them. Someone offered him money, but he declined. "Not today, Michael wouldn't have wanted it that way," he said. Sean enacted a kind of dual presentation during his walk—offering himself as a guardian of Michael's spirit as well as the embodiment of a particular Michael Jackson persona—he was at once both a Michael Jackson and Sean Vezina. The glasses and hat, the oxford-style shirt, the blazer and armband, all spanning 25 years of the MJ style lexicon, indicated to onlookers that they may approach him as if he *is* Michael Jackson, complete with the expectation that the impersonator will exhibit Jackson's voice and behavior as well.

Sean engaged in a kind of role-interchange performance, moving freely between his own identity and the Michael Jackson character. He used his own voice to communicate with people, receiving their condolences for Michael Jackson's death as himself, as if he was standing outside of the physical body he was dressed as and represented.

That is Sean's milieu, the transitional space between received identity—the thing forged by personal and cultural history—and aspirational self-creation. Walking the Boulevard, he engaged in this fluid role-interchange performance. He expressed his own grief and sense of loss both to, and with, the fans, all while posing for photos with them, in character, as Michael Jackson. And he played the role of Michael Jackson walking among the fans despite his recent death. True L.O.V.E.

Those moments with Melissa and Kevin and Sean, the elusive instances when the barrier between performance and self slipped, intrigued and unsettled me. The sidewalks of Harlem and Hollywood changed the way I think—not only about taking photographs—but also about identity, race, gender, and the ways in which we construct these from all the artifacts and memes and images and sounds of culture.

Having been an art student in the 1990s, I came of age immersed in the language of

Kirby Shields displays a personal tribute to Michael Jackson outside of the Staples Center during the memorial.

literary theory. My intellectual development involved seeing gender as fluid, believing fixed notions of race to be mistaken, and understanding identity as a constructed narrative. So, these notions were not new or foreign to me when I began to photograph the Michael Jacksons. But watching the representers embody and perform those ideas without this consciousness, and seeing the ways in which Michael Jackson moved people to liberate themselves from cultural constraints with agency, gave abstract ideas about liberation new heft and meaning. I see more clearly now what Walt Whitman meant when he wrote, "I contradict myself; I contain multitudes." We do. All of us. And certainly Michael Jackson did, perhaps quite a lot more than most.

CHAPTER FIVE

"Katherine Jackson was in tears when she saw him."
How Representers Construct Their Michael Jackson

 ased on the photo of Melissa and Kevin on Hollywood Boulevard, and the unusual moment of transcendence I witnessed there, I sought out other Michael Jackson impersonators in Los Angeles to photograph them, but this time in a controlled studio setting. An Internet search revealed sites like Gigsalad and Gigmasters, which allow users to search and hire celebrity lookalikes, impersonators, or tribute artists for parties or special events. While some impersonators charged upwards of $400 an hour, others did not specify a rate. I wrote to anyone I could find who described themselves in a way that implied they were a professional Michael Jackson performer.

I also posted an ad on Craigslist under the category of *gigs*. My ad simply stated:

> I'm looking for a Michael Jackson impersonator for a photography project. In exchange for two to three hours of your time, you'll receive $75 plus digital copies of any of the photos taken during the shoot.

I received one response after posting on Gigsalad, and three responses from a Craigslist post. I followed up on all of them. The Gigsalad contact didn't developed into anything. The performer's manager emailed me, and when I revealed what I was doing and that I could only offer the impersonator $75, plus digital files of the photo shoot, I received no reply. However, the Craigslist contacts proved much more encouraging. In all three cases, I was able to set dates and times for the impersonators to visit my house in the Los Feliz neighborhood of Los Angeles, where I had converted the living room into a shooting studio outfitted with a black velvet backdrop and a strobe kit.

The Michael Jacksons photography sessions continued for three years, first in Los Angeles, then in New York City, and then in the southeast and southwestern parts of the United States. In total, I photographed thirty-five people working as lookalikes, impersonators, or tribute artists.

WHO, WHAT, AND WHERE

In the aftermath of Michael Jackson's death, my quest to photograph professional Michael Jackson lookalikes, impersonators, and tribute artists evolved into a multi-year, multi-city project that included collecting and interpreting the impersonators' stories in an attempt to evaluate an emerging subculture within the world of professional mimicry. The research I have conducted among this group—the Michaels Jacksons—included extended interviews, participant-observation field work, and a survey with many of those who were photographed as well as other Michael Jackson representers who fell outside of the physical boundaries of the project (that is to say, outside of New York, Los Angeles, Las Vegas, the southwest and the southeast United States). As with much social documentary work, it has proven difficult for me to know where to mark the end of the research period and the start of the analysis process. As I write this, I am still meeting new Michael Jacksons and following many of their stories; I am still researching and documenting this emerging subculture.

The initial goal of this project had been to identify, document, and describe a growing subcultural phenomenon within popular culture. I wanted to observe individuals who self identify as Michael Jackson impersonators, lookalikes, and tribute artists. I wanted document the rites, language, and culture of a phenomenon that first emerged in June 2009. However, it is clear that in the period I have been conducting this work (2009–2013), the community of Michael Jackson impersonators has begun taking on a new shape, thanks, in part, to a gradual postmortem canonization process. With time, and emotional distance, the morally challenging aspects of Michael Jackson's life are being discarded. The controversies related to what some interpreted as his attempt to "change" his racial identity, the denial of his "blackness," the questions regarding his sexuality, charges of child molestation, and the related trials of the early 1990s and 2000s, are growing fainter. In the absence of the tragically flawed, physical person of Michael Jackson himself, only he towering images of an iconic performer—the song-and-dance persona and the humanitarian—remain. Popular TV talent shows like *American Idol, The Voice, Dancing with the Stars, America's Next Top Model*, have featured special episodes centered on

Michael Jackson; and in the fashion world, Irish milliner Phillip Treacy used Jackson's post-Thriller-era costumes as inspiration for his spring 2013 line of headwear. All of this indicates the extent of the reformation, rehabilitation, and re-examination of Michael Jackson's work.

For the most part, the Michael Jackson representers included in this work report that while growing up they were greatly influenced by Michael Jackson's music, his performances, his video personas—and his overarching message of inclusiveness and love. They grew up with his image, and his music infused into the very texture of their lives. They bore witness to Michael Jackson's career and life during formative periods of their own lives. Their personal histories are entwined with Michael Jackson's life and his story, and their associations and memories link them to one another in ways that will be impossible for representers thirty, twenty, or even ten years from now to understand.

While the Michael Jacksons in my study range in age from 19 to 51, the larger community of performers comes from an even broader age range and from far more dispersed geographical locations. I have observed professional Michael Jackson representers ranging from 8 to 55 years of age. But, the majority of representers documented here are in their 20s and early-to-mid 30s. They are both male and female and come from many racial and ethnic backgrounds. In addition, an extensive search and outreach indicates that there are individuals from the Philippines, Haiti, Pakistan, Guatemala, Colombia, Cuba, China, India, Russia, Paraguay, Peru, Brazil, Australia, Belgium, Hungary, Malaysia, New Zealand, Mexico, Serbia, Italy, Chile, and Sweden also identify themselves as Michael Jackson representers.

THE FORMS OF REPRESENTATION

While all representers shape their practice of Michael Jackson differently, and forge their representation based on their own social histories, psychological backgrounds and physical legacies, certain commonalities and distinctions emerged in my observation. This study has identified three broad classes of representers—*lookalikes*, *impersonators*, and *tribute artists*.[1]

A *lookalike* bears a strong natural resemblance to Michael Jackson. This type of performer is typically hired for an event, such as a party or a convention, to perform particular functions such as welcoming guests and shaking hands for a "meet-'n-greet" or posing for photos with attendees. Sometimes the lookalike will simply walk around an event in character. The lookalike's presentation relies on the physical resemblance to Michael Jackson and the quality of the costume. A lookalike isn't expected to sing and dance, instead, she or he may simply repeat lines or stock phrases generally associated with Michael Jackson as a part of the "performance."

Similar to a lookalike, an *impersonator* often also bears a natural resemblance to Michael Jackson. These performers may have a similar facial structure or physical build evocative of Michael Jackson. The impersonator may then enhance these natural similarities with character-appropriate clothing, make-up, and practiced mannerisms.[2] They sometimes refer to themselves as "illusionists." An impersonator employs a skilled use of character in his or her performance, and might incorporate some singing, dancing, and more character-appropriate language. These performers generally have spent a great deal of time studying the object of their mimicry and may bring some of their own interpretation into the performance. They may embellish their apparel with elements that aren't necessarily precise to the original, but are similar in style and sensibility. Such performers may even modify standard dance routines or song interpretations. This imbues the performance with a more spontaneous and natural air. As the impersonator's performance is more comprehensive, they usually receive a higher appearance fee than a lookalike.

The third level, the *tribute artist*, possesses a great deal of representational skill and may sometimes command a rate of pay equal to, or greater than, that of an impersonator. While about fifty percent of the representers surveyed referred to themselves as *impersonators*, most will, in an interview context, call themselves *tribute artists*. For many representers, the term *impersonator* carries a negative connotation, whereas the term *tribute artist* implies a high level of professionalism while simultaneously expressing a devotion, or deep admiration, for their subject. In addition, by identifying as a *tribute artist*, a *representer* is freed to explore their Michael Jackson performances more fully, and in more individualistic ways, than *lookalikes* and *impersonators*—they are, after all, *paying tribute*. While clearly based upon the Michael Jackson persona, tribute artists often appear liberated from direct comparisons to the actual performer. Furthermore, tribute artists are often considered more sophisticated in how they prepare their performances, costumes, make-up, and wigs. The perception is that they conduct their business in a highly professional manner, hold themselves to a higher standard of performance and behavior, and are especially mindful of the Michael Jackson brand as represented through their work.

IN PUBLIC / DEFINING THE FORUMS

An objective uniting all classes of representers is the intent to perform their interpretation of Michael Jackson before an audience. The audience provides validation of the conceptual and physical framework offered in the performer's representation. In this case, the imaginative and physical space the audience and the performer inhabit builds an authentic, shared cultural experience, bridging the intellectual gap between Michael Jackson—the actual person and entertainer—and the repres, the represent and his or her performance of Michael Jackson. Without a receptive and participating audience, the act is rendered meaningless, and the gap between concept and execution, between idea and actualization, between private fantasy and a shared celebration, cannot be spanned.

Performance spaces vary greatly, and all levels of the Michael Jackson representers have their venues—from the streets of Hollywood and Times Square to theaters that seat thousands. Each forum reveals a unique set of negotiations and expectations between performer and audience; and each performer in each forum creates a new Michael Jackson. In fact, the locus of the performance space helps to further refine the definitions of the Michael Jacksons:

HIGH-PRESENTER (High-Level Execution/High Visibility)

This group, for the most part, is comprised of impersonators, but may also include a small number of tribute artists whose performances are technically exact in replicating Michael Jackson's choreography. Notably, these performers don't sing, and they play to large audiences on a regular basis during extended runs in large venues. Examples of this stratum include performers employed by Las Vegas stage shows or high-profile extravaganzas like the Cirque du Soleil show *IMMORTAL*. These performers may have a slight physical build—like Michael Jackson's—or they may be more muscular, though this would be obscured within billowing clothing. They are usually costumed in a very authentic wardrobe created by a dresser or stage tailor. They often employ a wig, and don the ubiquitous black fedora. Of course, make-up is very important to a performer at this level as it helps support the Michael Jackson illusion; however, it may be simplified and highlight only key elements that are broadly, and easily, recognizable from afar as features of the Michael Jackson character: eyebrows and sideburns may be shaped into arches and darkened, lips reddened, a cleft in the chin may be added superficially, and eyelids and rims are lined in black. Because these performers are generally at a distance from the audience, they don't need to accentuate or define subtle facial features.

INTERMEDIATE-PRESENTER (Mid-Level Execution, High- To Mid-Level Visibility)

Primarily tribute artists, representers at this level can include impersonators—particularly those who are rising through the ranks of professional Michael Jackson performers. Intermediate-presenters seek opportunities to perform before various audiences as they hone their craft and professional skills. Regardless, representers at this level make their living entirely through their performances. They may perform at parties and conventions and command appearance fees that range from $300 to $500 a show. Many intermediate-presenters have career support in the form of an agent or manager. Intermediate-presenters are generally technically adept dancers, and they may sing or lip-synch as a part of their performance. They wear high-quality costumes, made of expensive materials that rival the aesthetics and style of Michael Jackson's own costumes. The intermediate-presenter's clothing may be custom-made or purchased from costumers who specifically create such replicas with exacting detail. The key difference between performers working at this level and high-presenters is that the costumes—hat, shoes, glasses, and other related accessories worn in performance—will be used multiple times in multiple venues, rather than in one dedicated outlet.

TRANSITIONAL-PRESENTER (Mid-Level Execution/Mid-Level Visibility)
Representers from this stratum are often from both the impersonator and tribute artist classes, and one of two things can be understood about them:

1) Either they are just beginning their work as professional Michael Jackson performers and will reinvest their income into the process, upgrading their clothing and accessories, dedicating more time to their craft, and developing their choreography and related performance skills with hopes of moving to a higher level of visibility; or

2) They are not "strata climbing" and plan only brief careers as Michael Jackson impersonators while they acquiring experience to be applied towards other kinds of performances or in a related field such as entertainment management. Transitional presenters work birthday parties and small events with a local profile; they also self-promote and employ no secondary support staff to manage their careers.

Consequently, transitional presenters work sporadically, not nightly like high-presenters, though they may have consistent gigs on a week-to-week basis. Because transitional presenters perform in various, and often unlikely, places, and due to the close proximity of the performer to the audience, each audience possesses a different set of expectations about the possibilities of interacting with the performer. A much more direct verbal and imaginative exchange flows between audience and performer in these situations, and much more is required of the performer in this setting as she or he transitions between the various roles of "representer as performer" to "representer as Michael Jackson persona," and even to "representer as self", meaning moments when a performer is acting as themselves though they are dressed as Michael Jackson and are in a performance context.

NEO-PRESENTER (Low-Level Execution/Low-Level Visibility)

Those at the neo-presenter level are usually at the very beginning of their careers as an impersonators or tribute artists and may aspire to rise into higher strata, or if they are lookalikes, they will likely remain in that classification. Someone working at this level generally does not perform as a dancer or singer in public, and may only bear a suggestive resemblance to Michael Jackson. Costume and make-up—the development of the visual persona—is more interpretive in this stratum. Neo-presenters might purchase their clothes from a variety of thrift stores, used-clothing stores, dedicated discount costumers, or eBay. These garments will be adapted to suit their own construction of the Michael Jackson persona. For example, one neo-presenter's primary costume consists of a black cotton military-style jacket adorned with silver chains and charms—a small fork, a small knife, and a small spoon—not standard gear that immediately evokes Michael Jackson. Given that performance is an infusion of the performer's self into the Michael Jackson character, there is a strong tendency for the neo-presenter to engage in a role-interchange performance, "representer as performer," "representer as persona," "representer as self" as he or she interacts with an audience. A neo-presenter might be hired to appear at a local event intended to serve a small audience, or may be a self-employed street performer on the sidewalks around Hollywood Boulevard, Times Square, or the Las Vegas Strip.

CHARACTER CONSTRUCTION

Michael Jackson's career spanned from the late 1960s to June 2009. Every one of his ten studio albums, every video, every public appearance, and every recorded performance provides a wealth of source material for Michael Jackson representers. Michael Jacksons at all levels commonly choose up to three videos, appearances, or performances around which they build their repertoire, though some focus on just one distinct image.

What motivates a performer to embody a particular Michael Jackson era is unique for each representer and may be based in something strongly personal, or even nostalgic; it may even be something the performer cannot specify. But many respondents to our survey identified a specific childhood experience—the memory of a Michael Jackson performance on TV, the first time they saw one of his videos, or a televised interview as the reason they chose to represent him in the first place. Often mentioned is Michael Jackson's interview on *Oprah* in 1993, the 1995 HBO concert film, *One Night Only*, or the Motown 25th anniversary celebration in March of 1983, when he first moonwalked in public. Regardless, once a performer selects an era to represent, he or she must then choose what he or she will perform and how to construct that performance—how the interpretation will appear for an audience. Impersonators and tribute artists have the added task of trying to move and sound like Michael Jackson. Many return to that initial inspiration—*that* video, *that* TV appearance, or *that* stage performance—as a starting point. The albums *Bad*, *Dangerous*, and *Thriller* stand as the most common source material amongst representers at all performance levels. "Thriller," "Beat It," "Billie Jean," and "Smooth Criminal" remain the songs most often performed.

In further discussions about their motivations for entering into the life of Michael Jackson representers, many note an initial moment of external acknowledgement, or validation, from an audience. Ten representers interviewed for this project report that they participated in a talent show and performed a Michael Jackson dance routine, and they either won the contest or received sufficient positive feedback to pursue their interpretation into the next level. They invested in the process and built costumes, thus migrating from amateur fan to neo-presenter status. Some remain at that level, lacking the confidence and experience to advance, while some proceed on to the higher performance strata, gaining access to larger audiences and better money, a good portion of which will be reinvested for more, and higher-quality, outfits.

NAMING + IDENTITY

Michael Jackson tribute artists and impersonators may consider themselves ambassadors for the Michael Jackson brand. While not officially employed by a commercial entity related to Michael Jackson, representers see themselves as custodians of Michael Jackson's legacy and are careful to develop their own persona in a manner that respects and promotes Michael Jackson as an entertainment entity as well as a human being. In keeping with this sensibility, representers put an enormous amount of thought and effort into developing all aspects of their interpretations and performances, including their stage names.

The names representers choose—and any titles they self-apply—are crafted to communicate both a desired kinship to Michael Jackson and the performer's own credibility, or brand, within the community of Michael Jacksons. For example, Omar Rajpute calls himself, "The Prince of Pop," an allusion to Michael Jackson's self-ascribed title, "The King of Pop." Rajpute promotes himself as heir apparent to Michael Jackson's work and adopted this name to communicate this ambition to others, as well as to promote his act. Many performers construct their nom-de-stage from an amalgam of their given name and their interpretation of Michael Jackson. A good example is Dominique Wilson, a female tribute artist living and working in Newark, New Jersey, who goes by the stage name "Mikette," a name that communicates her affection for Michael Jackson as well as her gender. Another popular style is to add or insert "MJ" into one's existing moniker.

In terms of the performance hierarchy, representers working at the high and intermediate levels are more likely to use their own names to describe their status in relation to other representers. Omar Rajpute's moniker "The Prince of Pop" communicates to potential employers, and the public, the level of authenticity he strives to achieve in his representation. Other representers at these levels will often attach a description of the quality of their performance next to it (i.e., Michael Kiss: "The #1 Michael Jackson Tribute Performer.")

The performer may also attempt to convey his or her authenticity and credibility by associating her or his stage name and representation with some form of validation, or endorsement, from the Jackson family, or even Michael Jackson himself. For example, Carlo Riley is a high-presenter who undertook a multi-city U.S. tour in the summer of 2012. His assistant Brenda Kelly describes Carlo Riley as being so genuine that Michael Jackson's mother herself was moved by his performance.

"Katherine Jackson was in tears when she saw him," Brenda enthused.

The representer's holy grail, of course, is Michael Jackson's own endorsement. For a tribute artist or impersonator, a direct Michael Jackson endorsement can take many different forms and be framed in various ways; and performers are not shy about publicizing any possible validation, even if it may seem tenuous. Representer Pete Carter of Los Angeles, describes himself on Gigsalad as "The Number ONE Michael Jackson Impersonator and Tribute Artist. . .And he has the real King of Pop's blessing" [sic]. Another representer who goes only by the name "Michael Jackson Tribute" in Richmond, Virginia, identifies himself as "The ONLY tribute artist to have performed live in concert with Michael Jackson's THIS IS IT band!" Navi, a representer in the U.K. who, on his website, calls himself "The World's #1 Michael Jackson Tribute," claims "endorsement doesn't come any clearer than Michael Jackson himself applauding you, inviting you to Neverland, and using you on several occasions to promote albums/concerts or as a decoy." This type of authentication, or endorsement, as with the Jackson-related moniker, is designed to capture prospective clients' attention by signaling the level of quality to be expected in a performance.

Commercial interests, while important in the self-naming process, are not the only factors at work here. Psychological and sociological aspects inform the renaming event as well. Across all cultures throughout human history, a common rite of passage delineating entry into a new phase of life, or into a new group, requires the individual to accept a new name. Christian confirmation rites and the tradition of women taking their husband's surname at marriage seem like clear examples. To cite less formal situations, consider the application of nicknames within friendship groups. In any event, as with entry into any new community or subculture, the representer's adoption of a new name communicates her or his willingness to bond one's own identity with the image and identity of Michael Jackson. As much as anything representers do, this signifies that they have joined the group. Like a tattoo, there is the presumption of permanence, and a sense of infusing one's self with Michael Jackson. It is an act of sacrifice, and a sublimation of one's original identity in favor of the representer's identity within the Michael Jacksons community.

Social media—specifically Facebook—has played a pivotal role in bringing tribute artists, impersonators, lookalikes, and super fans together, and even blurring these distinctions. Social media, in its immediacy and scope, offers a clear window into the culture of representers at the transitional and neo-presenter levels and the process of re-christening and re-identification that individuals go through as they are shaping their online hybrid identity. One need only open a Facebook page devoted to Michael Jackson to observe the breadth and scope of the renaming phenomenon: Raquel Jean-Joseph Jackson, LC Jackson, Sequin Jackson, Fray Jackson, Susie Dancer Jackson, HollywoodMJ Cristof, Miguel Angel Jackson, Apple G Jackson, Marine'chael Jackson, Marco Jackson; as well as the insertion of "MJ" as between real first and last name, Lamar MJ Coleman, and Perry "mj" Pullman.

CLOTHING + MAKE-UP.

The Michael Jackson character construction is a multi-step process. The search for, and acquisition of, appropriate clothing and the development of the make-up skills continue throughout the representer's career. These ongoing aspects of representation evolve as the representer becomes more involved in his or her work and as the performer gains confidence with public visibility and experience.

While visual authenticity, or looking as much like Michael Jackson as possible—

"Michaelesque," as one represser calls it—is a common aspiration, many represers base their appearance and act on more than one era, album, or video, even mixing styles from closely related eras and performances. For example, Devra Gregory, an impersonator from Los Angeles, sometimes performs in a red leather jacket similar to the one Michael Jackson wore in the 1983 "Thriller" video. She also performs in a white pinstripe suit, blue satin shirt, white tie, and fedora inspired by the video of "Smooth Criminal," a cut from the 1987 album *Bad*. At times, she may mix this standard outfit with the black sequined jacket from the "Billie Jean" video. No matter how she is attired, she wears a shoulder-length, Jheri curl wig resembling Michael Jackson's hair during the *Bad* era, roughly from 1986 to 1989. Even though Michael Jackson's hair changed in length, style, and fullness over time and from year to year, all of the represers indicate that they use just one wig, or style their own hair in just one way—usually flattened shoulder-length curls pulled back into a short ponytail, similar to the *Dangerous* era.

I witness the represers' desire for Michael Jackson verisimilitude up close during photo shoots. Represers are most impressed with photographs in which their appearance, facial expression, and posture all align with *their* ideal image of Michael Jackson. A term that comes up repeatedly when photographing intermediate and transitional-presenters is "illusion." These represers intend to create the illusion that Michael Jackson is present somehow, in some manner. When asked further to define what this means, the typical represser discusses the virtues of make-up, skillfully applied. For instance, Devra Gregory learned the basics of her make-up technique from female-to-male drag performers when she worked as a dancer in San Diego. She then practiced on her own for many months, attempting to transform her oval face into one resembling the angularity of Michael Jackson's. Her make-up application process takes over two hours. Devra's process, while clearly her own, exemplifies the time and devotion represers apply to their make-up craft in pursuit of the angular Michael Jackson visage they wish to present.

MJX, a Colombian transitional-level tribute artist who lives and works in suburban New Jersey, is very clear on how he wants people to perceive him. He always arrives in full make-up and costume for a performance, audition, or, in the case of working with me, a photo shoot. He reports that he spends about thirty to forty-five minutes applying make-up. The process radically changes the appearance of his face, eyebrows, and lips. He is in the business of creating an illusion, he says, and while he uses his own voice and talks freely about himself, he is very careful that no one that he works with in a professional capacity *sees* him in any other way than MJX, Michael Jackson Tribute Artist. Another performer,

Michael Knight of Woonsocket, Rhode Island, made me promise not to share his make-up secrets with any of the other representers, indicating that the technique he employs to emulate Michael Jackson's nose is proprietary. He believes that letting others know his craft could feed competition for work. Impersonators at the high, intermediate—and even some at the transitional levels—are keenly aware that the authenticity of their appearance distinguishes them from other representers, so make-up skills and their personal secrets are essential to their identity, brand, and business.

At the other end of the spectrum, we find representers like Dominique Wilson, an African-American tribute artist working at the neo-presenter level in Newark, New Jersey. She wears no make-up; instead, she emphasizes costuming and performance. She is not interested in creating an illusion through make-up or other craft. However, after our photo shoot, she complimented the photos that she believed expressed something of the "essence" of Michael Jackson we had captured in her facial expressions and posture. Regardless, Dominique says she seeks to emulate Michael Jackson's choreography and his generous spirit. When she started performing publicly in June of 2011, she purchased her costumes from a retailer in Hong Kong who sells Michael Jackson shirts, jackets, pants, and sparkly gloves on eBay. Now, Dominique, along with about forty percent of the tribute artists and impersonators surveyed, makes her own costumes, purchasing fabric and constructing outfits, or buying separate pieces that resemble something Michael Jackson would wear—white t-shirt, with a buttoned shirt, black pants, etc.—and coordinating her look.

Some costume elements are essential to every representer's interpretation of Michael Jackson—the black fedora, the sunglasses, the white glove—and these items, along with certain ornate beaded and sequined jackets, can be purchased at different levels of quality, depending on the performer's budget. For example, the white glove can range from $1,000 for a real white-leather golf glove covered with Swarovski crystals, to about 50 cents for a white nylon glove covered with flat, metallic-looking plastic discs. Between those extremes, gloves of various materials and different quality are all readily available through eBay for a wide range of prices.

Many purchase their gear online through a specialty company named Samantha Mo. Located in Udon Thani, Thailand, Samantha Mo operates two online outlets, samanthamo.com and michaeljacksoncelebrityclothing.com. They manufacture and market a range of outfits for ballroom, salsa, and cabaret dancing, as well as other sundry costumes. But far and away, they produce more replicas of Michael Jackson's shirts, pants, jackets, and arm wraps than any competitor. Samantha Mo also designs many items after his style. For a mass-produced Billie Jean-style jacket, a representer can pay as little as $49.99 for one with the plastic sequin discs pressed on the fabric, or up to $189.99 for a jacket with actual sequins sewn directly on the jacket. Representers at the neo-presenter and transitional-presenter levels will likely purchase the less-expensive version, while intermediate-presenters will likely choose the more expensive "Pro Series" jacket, as the Samantha Mo site calls it. As MJX claims, the more expensive garment helps conjure the illusion he is creating. "That," he said, "is my real job."

RACE + RACIAL IDENTITY.

A final, significant component to the persona any Michael Jackson representer forges is race—or skin tone. This is a unique dilemma for Michael Jackson tribute artists, impersonators, and lookalikes. It is worth considering that while Elvis Presley impersonators also come from the multitude of ethnicities and races, there is never any question that the figure they emulate was Caucasian, and he never meant to be anything but Caucasian. Elvis impersonators also may perform various periods of his life, but the choices available have to do with clothing style and, perhaps, girth, never race, as it relates to the Elvis's skin tone or facial structure.

But in shaping *their* representation, Michael Jackson representers must choose how they will interpret not only the fashion and music of the era they embody, but Michael Jackson's race—or skin tone—during that period. For example, a darker skin tone Michael Jackson would likely signify the *Off the Wall* to *Thriller* era, while lighter skin corresponds to the *Dangerous* era, and beyond. Consequently, African-American and other darker-skinned representers often lighten their faces and hands with make-up, and Caucasian representers may employ shadowing and foundation to shape their features. It is worth noting that these performers do not modify their natural skin color significantly; they simply adjust the color with make-up.

Despite this, without exception, the representers surveyed and interviewed agreed that Michael Jackson was an African-American man and performer; but for most of them, this is as far as the discussion of his race and ethnicity goes. When asked specifically whether Michael Jackson's race is an important part of playing the Michael Jackson character or representing Michael Jackson, all of the respondents said no. "I'm mixed-race," wrote one anonymous respondent. "Being mixed allows me to transition through his eras and appreciate all races. Like Michael, I find the beauty in all races and ethnicities." Another wrote, "I am Mexican and I don't think race is important part for being MJ cause he used to represent all cultures and races from the world [sic]. He is the only man who can be black and white at the same time and that's so beautiful."

There is no unified perspective on the exact tone of Michael Jackson's skin when it was in its lighter stages. Unlike the industry that has developed around his costuming, there is no company that sells Michael Jackson foundation, powder, eyeliner, and highlighting kits. There are, however, a number of online tutorials on how to use common drugstore make up to achieve large, wide-open looking eyes; to shape and shade cheekbones where there may be none; to give shape to a nose so that it appears thin and delicate with a finely pointed tip; and to create the illusion of a certain fullness to the sides of the nose around the nostrils. Devra Gregory has also developed a DVD tutorial on her make-up techniques that she has available for sale to other representers.

With very few exceptions, Michael Jackson is represented as his light-skinned version. Most representers at all levels shade their skin towards a version of Michael Jackson from between 1988 and 1993, no matter what era they actually portray, or what songs they perform. A consequence of this is that the light-skinned, race-neutral and gender ambiguous version of Michael Jackson prevails, even when paired with clothing and wigs and music from the earlier periods, when he was simply perceived as a young, black man. In many ways, through the agency of his representers, Michael Jackson has become a universal being, a thing writing itself over and over by the same sort of will over nature he exemplified.

CHAPTER SIX

"How do I look right now? Do I look like Michael Jackson?"
Narratives of Representers

n the more than three years I spent meeting, photographing, observing, and getting to know Michael Jackson representers, it has been a privilege and pleasure to share in very personal moments with many of my subjects. Their personal lives and work lives are as diverse as any cross section of any population, but they share one common goal—the continuation and proliferation of Michael Jackson's work and his presence in our cultural consciousness. In the following pages, I will delve deeper into six of these individual's lives. Unfortunately, due the constraints of time and space, we cannot truly and *fully* explore even the six representers here, let alone the equally compelling tales of so many more who generously invited me into their worlds. I can only thank them all for their kindness, courage, and trust.

SEAN VEZINA

Sean Vezina worked on Hollywood Boulevard, where I first met him in 2007. After watching him perform there, I struck up a conversation and eventually photographed him performing on the sidewalk. When we reconnected after the Los Angeles memorial in 2009, I photographed him in front of Jimmy Kimmel's theater on Hollywood Boulevard, that sets of photos, along with the ones of Melissa and Kevin, were the first of what would become "The Michael Jacksons". At the time, however, I was just hoping to learn about the lives of the celebrity street performers on Hollywood and Highland. Even without the larger frame of the Michael Jackson represented community, his story intrigued me.

Sean is Caucasian and grew up in as an adopted child in Santa Cruz, California. In 1995,

Sean saw Michael Jackson on TV, and inspired by what he saw, taught himself to dance. He practiced all of Michael Jackson's moves, and when he felt he was proficient enough, he went from door to door in his neighborhood and asked people if he could dance as Michael Jackson for them in exchange for money.

"No one said yes," he told me.

When he graduated from high school in 1999, Sean hit the road. For over a decade, he traveled between Los Angeles and Las Vegas, performing on the Strip and Hollywood Boulevard, and in small towns along the way as he hitchhiked between the two cities.

Sean presents an amalgam Michael Jackson persona—a sort of generalized Michael Jackson. He fashioned his outfit from thrift-store finds, and he doesn't seek to emulate the look of a particular video or performance He wears a black wig purchased from one of the costume stores on Hollywood and Vine, a black fedora one size too large so that it fits over the wig, and mirrored sunglasses. He looks nothing like Michael Jackson naturally, and his clothing only suggests his referent, but he does augment his appearance with make-up. In this case it's not foundation and powder, or anything to lighten or darken his skin tone. Instead, he uses a permanent black marker to line his piercingly blue eyes and to draw in sideburns and eyebrows. It's the right color, he told me, and doesn't smudge or come off for days.

Sean's strategy for working the boulevard was to walk around as Michael Jackson and to interact with people, seeking "donations" for his performance. He sometimes brought a radio and would perform modified dance routines based on Michael Jackson's videos, as when we first met. In a twelve-or-more-hour day, Sean will be lucky to earn $30, five to ten dollars of which he spends at the Subway or McDonalds on Franklin Avenue on the way to the grassy park and picnic benches of the Hollywood Bowl where he sometimes slept.

In August of 2012, Sean, like many other MJ tribute artists, visited New York City to attend Spike Lee's Michael Jackson birthday celebration in Prospect Park which was scheduled for Saturday, August 25th.

DEVRA GREGORY

In 2009, after initiating the deliberate process of documenting the Michael Jacksons, the first impersonator I booked for a photo shoot was a 51-year-old Caucasian woman named Devra Gregory. She goes by "Dev" or "Dev as MJ" when in the Michael Jackson character. Dev lives in San Diego and sometimes performs in Los Angeles. Eventually, we scheduled the shoot to coordinate with one of her Hollywood performances. She arrived around 1p.m. on a Friday afternoon and spent two hours applying heavy make-up that radically transformed her face. When she emerged from her make-up process, she had the appearance of a small fine nose, an angular face, and a sharp jaw line. Dev brought four outfits with her and two large duffle bags filled with supporting materials—pants, shoes, socks, gloves, black fedora—the items that complete the transformation into her own interpretation of Michael Jackson. Dev's image and her act centered around two eras— *Thriller*, from 1983, and *Dangerous*, from 1991.

When she first stepped in front of my camera, Dev wore a red jacket, white t shirt, and black pants—an outfit modeled after Michael Jackson's attire in the "Beat It" music video. At first, we struggled a bit to find a rhythm as photographer and subject. I had an idea of what I wanted from her—a static portrait born of a moment when she was mentally focused in her portrayal of Michael Jackson, where she revealed the physical construction of her character. But Dev but insisted on presenting Michael Jackson as a physical performance. Our work together became something of a push and pull between these two modes. She performed her Michael Jackson moves—spinning, turning, stopping *en pointe*, and then extending one arm above her left shoulder and ear while the other pointed to the ground—and I tried to capture her at moments where she broke through and presented an interpretation of the character she portrayed, not the performer Michael Jackson.

At times during the shoot, my objective seemed impossible to achieve. She had engaged, and fulfilled, her Michael Jackson character transformation ritual—applying the makeup, preparing her body, binding her breasts to flatten them beneath her t-shirt, grooming her outfits to ensure that all the sequins and emblems were in place and the armband was placed in the right location on the upper arm of her jacket. For her, the next step, of course, was to engage in her usual performance of Michael Jackson. My request as a photographer subverted that last step; I was asking her to deconstruct, if not eliminate, the way she portrayed Michael Jackson. I asked her to be Devra in Michael Jackson costume. But because she had constructed Michael Jackson in a methodological way, her portrayal— unlike Melissa, Kevin and Sean—only existed on stage where she was Dev, a persona removed from Devra. She did not slide effortlessly between herself in costume and her role as Michael Jackson.

Dev's construction and execution was intended be as Michael Jackson the performer. To Dev—who comes from a ballet tradition and got into Michael Jackson after learning female-to-male drag from lesbian cabaret performers—the intent of her preparation was to dance as Michael Jackson on a stage in front of an audience. After the onstage performance she could shift into a degree of characterization while mingling with audience members and posing for photographs, but in these situations she, like Sean, was really Dev in the costume of Michael Jackson. In the context of a photo shoot in my living room, she was again performing, but what I wanted was that she portray her version of the Michael Jackson character, and separate herself from the dance performance.

After about an hour of photographing and dancing and posing, she changed her outfit to a black blazer with a short-sleeved, white, V-neck t-shirt underneath. She had put on black pants with a silver stripe down each side. Still looking to find something about her that might be unexpected, or a moment that was the perfect fusion of her and her portrayal of Michael Jackson, I asked her to take her jacket off. Her t-shirt hung more heavily than I expected, so I asked her about it. She said that she takes two Fruit of the Loom, V-neck t-shirts and sews them together to disguise her breasts and the binding she wraps around her body. Her arms were covered with freckles, a detail that surprised me. I couldn't remember what she looked like when she had arrived before her makeup application transformed her skin to a smooth and uniform pigmentation.

My assistant, Jenny, suggested that Dev fold her arms in front of her. Dev complied, and I started photographing; she stayed more or less still, while I refocused and moved, just slightly, after each shot. It was a brief interlude. Dev then began another performance sequence with another outfit. It wasn't until she left that I reviewed the photos and found, among the 300-plus images I took that afternoon, a single image uniting the elements of her unique personal portrayal of Michael Jackson and the Michael Jackson character. But that one image captured the uncanny quality I had seen at times with Sean Vezina, and with Melissa and Kevin on Hollywood Boulevard. It began to seem that there was an element that unified these performers in the context of the photo shoot—a moment, however fleeting, when the essence of their individuality was visible through the Michael Jackson visage.

JOVAN RAMEAU

Jovan Rameau, another Hollywood Boulevard Michael Jackson, is in many ways Sean Vezina's opposite. It is not just race, but socio-economics and education that cast them in stark relief to one another. Jovan has an MFA from the Institute of Advanced Theater Training at Harvard and makes a decent living as a represeter, who, in late 2011, was supporting both himself *and* his girlfriend. The Michael Jackson star on the Walk of Fame is his anchor, and he's there from 9 a.m. until 11 p.m., three days a week, Thursday, Saturday and Sunday, posing for pictures with tourists. Though he's a lookalike and builds his Michael Jackson character from a very particular set of "Thriller" video references, he is much more interested in capturing what he calls "the spirit of Michael Jackson" than in precisely replicating his '80s look. Even so, his costume is unassailable; his red leather jacket, white sequined glove, low-slung red belt and rhinestone leg band, are just the right details for the '80s Michael Jackson he presents. He is a true lookalike; his features, frame, and gestures are convincingly Michaelesque. But Jovan's skin color does not entirely resemble either the medium-brown complexion of the young Michael Jackson, or the pale tones for which he drew so much scorn during the latter part of his life. And that has proven to be provocative and disturbing for both Jovan and his audience.

I met Jovan in March of 2010 when he came to my studio in Los Feliz to be photographed for this project. A year later, I asked him to appear in a short video piece. I had hired a make-up artist, and I filmed Jovan while she applied the make-up that transformed him into his Michael Jackson character. At the end of the shoot, he started to leave in full costume and make-up, and I asked him where he was going.

"To Hollywood Boulevard," he said, "I don't want to waste a good make-up job."

This opened up the subject to me, and I asked Jovan about his experiences working as a Michael Jackson impersonator; something that we only briefly touched on when we first met. In 2010, he was not working on Hollywood Boulevard. At that time he was between trips—one to Fiji, and the other to South Africa—both in support of his work as a Michael Jackson lookalike. His employers paid for these trips, and that gave him great confidence. He even showed me a copy of *The Fiji Sun*, a local newspaper, that ran an article about his visit with a photograph of him surrounded by children from the Ratu Navula Secondary School.

But now, he was back in the United States, and working on Hollywood Boulevard. "How *is* that?" I asked. He lowered head slightly, which I read as embarrassment and defeat. Jovan told me about putting together a one-man show depicting his experiences as a Haitian immigrant struggling for work as an actor and making ends meet as a Michael Jackson lookalike. It would be titled *Dancing in the Shadow*. This performance, he imagined, would be his ticket out of the impersonation business and into a "real acting career." He also told me that he was writing a book.

Jovan Rameau's relationship to Michael Jackson, and the interpretation of the Michael Jackson character he presents, are much different than many other represeters I have observed. His ambitions are different than most, and his attitude towards both Michael

Jackson and his own need to portray Michael Jackson is very complex and nuanced. When Jovan came to the U.S. from Haiti as a boy he saw Michael Jackson as "a black man who was widely admired by everyone." He took comfort in being recognized for his likeness to Michael Jackson and saw impersonating him as both a stepping stone to an acting career, and a way to liberate himself from what he describes as the confines of being black and Haitian in the U.S. His personal history and his cross-cultural awareness seem to have made Jovan keenly attuned to comments about blackness, skin-tone, and race—and to his own condition as an ambitious artist with independent aspirations who is dependent upon his Michael Jackson character to pay the bills.

I later arranged to meet Jovan on Hollywood Boulevard, to observe him as he worked. That morning, when I first saw Jovan, he was talking with a woman. He later told me that her name is Christine, and that she is a friend from his Harvard days. When they said good-bye, they hugged for a long time. After they finally separated, he turned to me, and telling me he would return shortly, he left. Ten minutes later he reappeared. "Seeing her brought up a lot of emotions," he said. Jovan had finished the acting program at USC ten years before, and after that he headed back east to get an MFA at Harvard.

"They always want to friend me on Facebook, but I decline," he said, referring to his friends from college and the Harvard MFA program. "I haven't made it yet and I don't want them to know that,"

This was why Jovan had to leave after seeing Christine; he was confused and embarrassed about working on the Boulevard, "play acting" as Michael Jackson.

Even though our acquaintance had begun over a year and a half before, Jovan had told me very little about certain aspects of his life, particularly if those details had to do with dates and times. He had not told me what year he left Haiti for the U.S., for example, nor had he ever told me his age. I concluded that he probably came to the U.S. in the late 1980s when he was a teenager. At some point, he worked as a busboy at a restaurant in Miami, and it was there that customers often told him he resembled Michael Jackson. At the time, he saw Michael Jackson as a black man who had gained the respect of white America and the country in general. That was important to him, because as a Haitian living in the U.S., he experienced a lot of disrespect, if not outright racism. He took comfort in the fact that so many people commented on his likeness to Michael Jackson, and he saw that acting and performing like Michael Jackson was a way to raise himself up and overcome the experiences of bigotry and racism that he endured.

Later, when Michael Jackson went through the various legal problems of the 1990s,

Jovan stopped performing his Michael Jackson in public and, on the advice of Dr. Joyce Brothers, whom he met in a professional capacity, went to college and studied acting. He graduated in 2000 and was soon cast to play the lead in a film about Marcus Garvey. He was set to receive $50,000 for the part, and all signs indicated that this was his big break. To celebrate, he brought his mother to the penthouse suite at the hotel in Miami where he had been a busboy all those years ago. Jovan saw the penthouse suite was a metaphor for his impending success, for his forthcoming journey upward. He thought about buying his mother a house, too, and that idea made him ecstatic.

Then Jovan heard a radio news report claiming that the actor Ben Vereen had been in an accident and had been hit by a car while walking in his Malibu neighborhood. Ben Vereen had been cast in the Marcus Garvey film as well, and he was probably one of the reasons the film received funding in the first place. Just like that, the project was put on hold. As Jovan revealed this to me, his sense of loss was palpable. Since then he had been waiting for another opportunity, and he believed he had found it with his one-man show.

Jovan was eloquent when it came to the issue of race, a discussion that I inevitably have with all of the Michael Jackson impersonators and tribute artists I have observed and interviewed. Jovan's skin is light medium-brown with golden undertones. It doesn't entirely resemble either the fairly dark skin tone of Michael Jackson's early years of fame, or the white skin of the latter part of his career. The make-up Jovan wears is designed to lighten his skin to resemble Michael Jackson in the late 80s, when his skin was lighter than it was in the 1970s or early 1980s, but not yet white. Jovan's wig, slightly curly, at a length just barely brushing the tops of his shoulders, also suggests that era. Because Jovan started portraying Michael Jackson, in part, to help liberate himself from what he described as the confines of being black and Haitian in the U.S., his experience on Hollywood Boulevard has become something of an exercise in monitoring people's responses to his portrayal of Michael Jackson's race, as much as it is about making money.

As people passed by, Jovan recounted the story of his life easily, relaying the disappointments of losing the Marcus Garvey movie and having to resort to these sidewalk performances with a great deal of emotion. It was moving to witness this, particularly given that we were on the very sidewalk that symbolized Jovan's defeats. People who continually approached and asked to have their pictures taken with him—as Michael Jackson—when Jovan clearly believes that he could have his own star on the Walk of Fame, and that strangers should want to have their picture taken with him—Jovan Rameau, surrounded us. Even though these interactions with Michael Jackson fans and tourists interrupted our conversation, and the exchanges distracted from the gravity of our conversation about his life, Jovan, the consummate professional, was able to maintain a consistent tone with me and the fans, quickly flowing from one context to the other.

Michael Jackson's star is the one most frequently visited and photographed on the Walk of Fame. As people pass they see Jovan, quickly recognize him as Michael Jackson, and then express a variety of responses. Typically, a tourist will comment on Jovan's likeness, "He looks *just* like Michael Jackson!" Then there may be a short period of silence while they assess his features and clothing very closely, as if carefully aligning his appearance with their own memory of Jackson. Others will look and laugh, "Oh wow! It's Michael Jackson!" These second types of responses are fraught with irony and a detached humor.

As Jovan stood by Michael Jackson's star during my midday visit at the end of October, the sun shone bright and strong and the air was warm. As the day progressed, it grew hot. Jovan's costume is layered—a red long-sleeved shirt covered by the red leather jacket. Some days, he told me, he wears a long-sleeved shirt with a lined wool jacket. On a typical day, when the sun is high above Michael Jackson's star, Jovan carefully orchestrates his movements, drifting slightly east down the sidewalk, and then returning when the sun has faded. If he didn't, he told me, the perspiration would collect across his forehead under the wig, and eventually drip down his face, ruining his make-up.

A group of three Americans approached Jovan as he straddled Michael Jackson's star, "May we take your picture?" one of them asked.

"Sure! For a three-dollar donation," he answered. One of the women nodded, and her two friends stepped directly up to Jovan and looked back towards her. She held the camera up and snapped the picture. Jovan suggested that they gather around Michael Jackson's star and instructed the two women to crouch down next to him on the sidewalk so their photographer friend could get the three of them into the frame. Jovan held his left hand out like a claw—a reference to *Thriller*—and prompted the girls to do the same as they all looked into the lens.

Unlike other the Michael Jackson impersonators on the boulevard, Jovan does not dance, he only poses for photographs. He is very conscious—if not self-conscious—of his appearance, particularly his face. When being photographed, Jovan angles his head down, showing the right side of his face towards the camera, since he believes this offers his most Michael Jackson-like side. He opens his eyes widely to make them appear as round as possible, juts his chin towards the camera so that his jaw line appears sharp and dramatic, and he refreshes his smile every second or two so his expression appears genuine. Jovan is aware of people's expectations; he knows that they expect to see "Michael" and that is what he wants to give them.

"How do I look?" he asked me as we talked that day. "Do I look like Michael right now?"

In the moments just before and after posing with "fans," as he calls them, Jovan is himself—he uses his own voice to negotiate the financial arrangements and to respond to comments about himself and Michael Jackson This can be confusing for the fans, who want to interact with Jovan as if he is Michael Jackson. To the fans, this undercuts their perception of Jovan as Michael Jackson and betrays the moment of play in which they had initially engaged. Jovan seems well aware of the cognitive dissonances at work and helps to smooth it with his graciousness, while remaining himself within the Michael Jackson character.

Jovan is very clear about his intention—he is an actor playing Michael Jackson within a very particular context, in this case, Hollywood Boulevard, where the boundaries between fantasy and reality are blurry at best.

When he is interacting with fans, is very generous with his time, giving them the opportunity for multiple pictures, as opposed to other performers on the block who only allow one picture, and possibly a safety shot, in case the first photo is somehow imperfect. There is a routine to each interaction—Jovan offers the amateur photographer instructions on where to stand in relation to him, then he shows her or him how to stand—hip out, crouched on the sidewalk next to the star, and their hands shaped like a claw. This can take anywhere from 45 seconds to three minutes, at a cost of three dollars.

Through experimentation and over time, Jovan has come to understand the psychology of the *three* dollars in this context. He used to ask for two, but another impersonator, Melinda, told him to ask for three.

"Two dollars is too little to ask for, and five dollars too much," she said, "but if you say three dollars, generally people don't have three single bills and will give you a five dollar bill, not expecting change back."

There is also the issue of perceived value, Jovan says. "People are willing to pay that extra dollar because they believe the value of what they will receive in return will be greater."

He has also noticed that people who appear to have a lot of money will give less, and people who appear to have less money will give him more. Occasionally, Japanese tourists will give him a tip of $50 to $100. Japanese people, he told me, love Michael Jackson. In fact, earlier that day, before I arrived—he had received a hundred dollar bill from a Japanese woman. She was going to give him $200, but her husband told her that $100 was just fine. Usually, he will make about $450 a day, but that day—because of the large tip—he would bring home $550.

Jovan planned to use the money he made over the weekend to help pay for *Dancing in the Shadow*, his one-man show. He planned to perform his show over three weeks in December 2011. His goal was to earn $8,000 by the end of November to finance the theater rental, director, and lighting designer. The day before we saw each other, Jovan signed a lease at the Lounge Theater on Santa Monica Boulevard for its use on three Thursday nights and three Sunday afternoons in December. He was almost breathless as he told me about it.

"Oh Lorena, this is going to be it! It's my ticket!" he said.

The show would be directed by his fiancé, Naomi, a 24-year-old woman from the Netherlands whom Jovan met on a tour at the Forest Lawn Cemetery, where Michael Jackson is buried. They fell in love, and she moved to the U.S. to be with Jovan. Naomi also acts, and Jovan supports her with his earnings from Hollywood Boulevard, and in turn, they support each other in their individual professional creative endeavors.

Jovan continued to work, chatting with tourists and collecting tips for the photos. He held a wad of bills in his hand. Visible on top was a ten-dollar bill, beneath it was a five, and then a thick wad of ones. I asked him why he kept the ten on top.

"Because then people will be more inclined to give me ten dollars. If they see a dollar, they will only give a dollar," he replied.

Even though he asks for a three-dollar tip, many people offer him money without asking first. Jovan carries a small brown satin bag slung over his left shoulder—Louis Vuitton, he tells me—that he bought at Goodwill for $20. Prior to finding the bag he had prayed to own something with the Vuitton brand name. The bag is stained and the clasp doesn't work. The money he collects ends up in the Vuitton bag when he is working on the star, but he has to press it under his arm tightly so that the money doesn't fall out. The bag is clearly visible in the pictures he takes with fans, but no one seems bothered by this. Like other characters and representers on Hollywood Boulevard, there are details in their costumes and presentation that are not in keeping with what is being represented—it is akin to breaking the fourth wall in film or in television shows, as if both parties say, "We agree to participate in this simulated experience, but will act as if it is an authentic interaction."

Working the Hollywood Walk of Fame, Jovan Rameau is a racial lightening rod, repeatedly evaluated, praised, criticized and condemned for the ways in which he performs Michael Jackson and represents blackness. He listens to passersby, absorbing their comments about Michael Jackson, about race, and about skin color. When someone makes such a comment, he often types it into his cellphone, character by character.

"You know," he says, "I have over two thousand quotes from people who pass by, and the fans come to see me here. I want to put together a book. A book of all the quotes I've heard from people who've said that I'm too black to be Michael Jackson."

"What have you heard?" I ask.

"Black people absolutely refuse me, saying that I'm too black, then they go (to be photographed) with the white Michael," he said, referring to another performer on Hollywood Boulevard.

"But the white people love me for my authenticity, and will come to be photographed with me over the light-skinned Michael. A white lady once said to me, 'You look like Michael Jackson from the days I want to remember him: Beautiful! Beautiful!'"[1]

Jovan calls his book a "documentary coffee table book," and sees this as another way to move out of the shadow of Michael Jackson's persona. As Jovan explained, in addition to quotes from passersby, his book will contain interviews with people he has met at Michael Jackson's star. He has questioned some visitors about their opinions of Michael Jackson and his race. Once, he met a psychologist from Melbourne, Australia, and when he asked her why the black people he encounters on the star strongly deny that Michael Jackson was black, she told him, "To black people, Michael was one of their own who achieved all these amazing things. When he changed his appearance and looked closer to white, they felt he abandoned them. The complexion of his children added insult to injury. So when they look at you, they say, 'You are not Michael Jackson, Michael was white,' because they feel hurt. They don't get the credit for Michael Jackson's greatness."[2]

As if on cue, an African-American man walked towards us on the sidewalk. He spat on the ground as he looked at Jovan and said, "Take the costume off! Remove that face and be yourself!" He then tapped his heart. This strikes at the core of Jovan's frustration with his life as a Michael Jackson. He recognizes, and is willing to participate in, the game of representation, but feels like he is losing himself in it.

When the man had disappeared in the crowd, Jovan said to me, "You know a lot of crazy people say a lot things, but I really ponder about these things. I thought that was very profound. It connects to what my show is about."

OMAR RAJPUTE

A month later, I arranged to photograph another Michael Jackson representer who had contacted me after seeing the Craigslist ad. Omar Rajpute, a 27-year-old Pakistani man, was driving in from where he lived in Irvine, California, about 40 miles from where I worked in Los Angeles, but due to traffic, the ride can take anywhere from two to four hours. It was a rainy day, too, which in L.A. causes massive slow downs. Omar arrived two hours late for our photo shoot, and he wasn't made up. He said didn't even own make-up, and usually went to the MAC cosmetics store to have one of the clerks there apply it for him. Suzanne, my assistant that day, and I quickly searched through what make-up we had and came up with a single black and brown eyeliner pencil and a tube of black mascara. Suzanne smeared the mascara on Omar's face forming a set of sideburns, and I added the eyeliner to his cheeks to help define the cheekbones and to create a cleft in his chin. I also defined the edge of his eyes.

Omar brought three Michael Jackson outfits and five solid ideas of how he wanted to be photographed. His first outfit consisted of a silver Lycra shirt and black pants. Around his waist he wrapped a six-inch thick black belt with a silver medallion-like buckle at the center. The buckle was about eight inches by eight inches and he placed it upside down on his torso. Omar called it a "wrestling belt," as it resembled something a champion wrestler or boxer might win in a title match. He had purchased it from a costume shop. As I photographed, Omar danced wildly and energetically, his arms cutting sharp and dynamic lines that brought him beyond the edges of my puny five-foot wide backdrop. Eventually, I gave him instruction on how keep the energy high, but to angle his arms forwards, towards me, and the camera so that they stayed within the frame and the backdrop.

The version of Michael Jackson Omar presented was primarily a performer, but it also had key elements of characterization. Omar was not interested in replicating the costumes and dance moves of Michael Jackson with the precise execution of Dev. Instead, Omar's costumes and choreography served as a foundation, upon which he built an entity reminiscent of Michael Jackson, but which pushed the boundaries of the persona, mashing it up with content from a multitude of cultural elements and scenarios. The silver outfit and upside-down wrestling belt are just one example. Omar's impulse to play with the available images and the various cultural touchstones that signify Michael Jackson was also apparent when he changed into the next outfit—a red jacket with gold buttons and gold embroidery under which he wore a white t-shirt with a "V" torn into the neck. He augmented this with a brace on his right forearm, similar to the one worn by Michael Jackson on the *Dangerous* and *HIStory* tours in the early 1990s. However, Omar covered most of it with the sleeve of the red jacket. Physically, Omar was aggressive. His dancing was technically well executed.

It was deliberate and athletic, but lacked the lightness and smoothness of Michael Jackson.

Sometime into our shoot, Omar broke for a moment and pulled something from his bag. "I brought this with me, and I was hoping you could take my picture as I hold it," he said. Then he held up a large stuffed ape for me to see. "You know, like when Michael Jackson had Bubbles the chimpanzee."

I never would have thought to bring, or add, such a prop to a shoot of this nature, but I was delighted to see he had such vision for his characterization. He put his left arm around the back of his Bubbles and brought it in close to his chest. With his dark aviator sunglasses and fedora on, and thick tendrils of hair hanging in his face, he angled his head to look down at it. His face was almost expressionless, but in the way his right hand held the toy's leg and the lightness of his right hand wrapped around its body, he communicated something unexpected—real affection. The actual Michael Jackson and Bubbles photo shoot occurred in the mid-1980s. Michael wore red and white satin pajamas and a dressing gown and Bubbles wore a light blue outfit. In the background, leaves and tree trunks hinted at nature. The real portrait was intended to illustrate the intimacy between human and human-like pet, implying that Michael Jackson—like the fictional Dr. Doolittle—possessed a magical quality that allowed him to transcend human boundaries and communicate with the animal kingdom. But Omar's version represented Michael Jackson from different eras and suggested that he had just stepped off stage. This scenario, Omar with "Bubbles," and a straightforward portrait of Omar sitting alone in a chair angled towards the camera were the strongest images from the shoot. Omar was a riveting performer, perhaps electric, but he tended to hide himself within his physical interpretation of Michael Jackson. His Michael Jackson was tall and imposing. He didn't sing, but he danced aggressively, and his face was expressionless, void of any intent or hope of selling his characterization to an audience. Again, it was in the moment of slippage between roles as character and performer, self-consciousness and immersion, that something clicked.

Omar Rajpute approaches his representation of Michael Jackson in a much different manner than most other Michael Jacksons I've encountered. And of all the representers with whom I have become acquainted and have interviewed, he has the most specific objectives. Omar, A.K.A., "The Prince of Pop," in a large, four-bedroom house with his parents. He identifies himself an impersonator and is a blend of a transitional and intermediate presenter—he makes some money performing locally, primarily in Orange County, though he also performs at private parties in Los Angeles, and, in the last couple of years he has worked in the New York City area on a regular basis. In addition, he has documented more than one million views of his Michael Jackson dance and music remixes on YouTube, and he has been on *America's Got Talent* and *So You Think You Can Dance*. He sees the work of Michael Jackson as an entity to be built upon. Omar's ultimate goal is to, "take Michael Jackson to a different level by adding flavor to it."

After our photo shoot, Omar and I maintained contact, and he invited me along to see one of his performances. So, on a Thursday evening in late October of 2011, I arrived at his house at 7 p.m., as he prepared for a performance later than night at *Hatam*, an Iranian restaurant in Mission Viejo. For some time, Omar had circulated flyers around south Orange County, and the owner saw one, contacted Omar, and invited him to perform regularly as Michael Jackson. Thus began one of Omar's steady gigs. The show I was to see would be on "Ladies' Night."

That evening, I sat in his bathroom and watched him apply his make-up. I had asked to interview him and spend time with him that night and he agreed to have me come along, but he seemed self-conscious and awkwardly formal. His tone and demeanor and the style of his storytelling made it clear he thought he was talking to a reporter. I remembered when Omar came over to my studio for his photo shoot—without make-up, and with no idea of how to apply make-up, and how my assistant and I had to put his face on for him with what we scrounged up. But standing in his bathroom that night, the sink covered with the dregs of last night's—last week's and last month's—foundation applications, it was clear that his make-up knowledge and skills had progressed.

"I feel that in my impersonation of him, I should really go all-out," he said as he applied the L'Oreal TruMatch foundation that he had started buying at Rite Aid. "I try to get the lightest make-up I can," he said, referring to the fair skin tone he achieved through the make-up.

As he told me his story, his voice warbled slightly as he stroked the foundation over his throat. Omar came to the U.S. when he was five years old, and even though he didn't speak English then, he learned to emulate Michael Jackson's dancing and earned himself an eponymous nickname. In 2002, when Omar was fifteen, he was visiting friends in Anaheim when his life suddenly changed. Anaheim was a rough place then, rife with gang activity and random violence. He was walking down the street when he was, randomly, shot in the neck. He remembers lying on the sidewalk, feeling blood rushing out of the wound in his neck, hoping that he would make it. Finally, in the distance he heard the sound of the ambulance and, he said, he knew he would pull through. The experience affected him profoundly. He returned to practicing Islam, and when he graduated from high school a few years later, he fully committed himself to becoming a Michael Jackson performer. He sees himself now as, "The best Michael Jackson dancer in the world."

Once the foundation layer was complete, he pressed light powder onto his face, including his lips. That Michael Jackson was African-American is a fact not lost on Omar. But what the issue of being an African-American has meant historically in the U.S., and what this could have meant to Michael Jackson and his work, is not at all a part of the consciousness Omar brings to his representation. He never mentions any race-related episodes, nor does he recount any comments about his own skin color.

After applying the foundation, Omar worked on his nose. He used black eyeliner along both sides of the bridge of his nose to make it seem thinner, but he doesn't bother to outline or shade in his nostrils to change their shape. He then applied the eyeliner to contour his cheeks, creating the illusion of more prominent cheekbones. The wig he had purchased from a wig-maker in Los Angeles seemed more scraggly than when he came for the photo shoot a year and a half before, and a residue of make-up and sweat had stained its edge. In addition, Omar's costume included a slightly crushed fedora, also bearing traces of foundation around its rim. But when Omar put on the hat and tilted it, all of the evidence of wear and age seemed to disappear.

For this appearance, Omar decided to wear his "Thriller" outfit. He pulled a red jacket from his closet. According to Omar, it is one of the first pieces of Michael Jackson clothing he bought. The sleeves were tattered and shredded, perfect for a rendition of "Thriller," and he pulled the lining out and cut the sleeves to the mid-forearm, ". . .to make it more "Thriller"-like." He pulled on a white t-shirt, gold sock coverings, and then a black Everlast arm brace of the type that Michael Jackson wore. He added a pair of frayed black pants and worn black shoes to complete his look.

During his pre-show preparations, Omar's parents arrived home. He spoke to them in Urdu, introducing me as his photographer as we stood in the large white kitchen. They were kind and hospitable, asking me if I'd like to sit down and have a drink. As we chatted I noted the opulence of Omar's home. The large kitchen was open to a living room with a high ceiling. Along the opposite walls a pair of ornate maroon couches were covered with a collection of frilly white pillows. The long narrow windows at the end of the room were topped with white half-curtains lined with white lace so dense it was difficult to see through. A fifty-six-inch television was mounted about five feet from the floor in between the impressive windows.

In English, Omar told his parents that we had to leave and we said good-bye. As we walked towards the street, Omar asked if I could drive.

"I don't have enough gas. I didn't have time to get it last night," he admitted. Omar explained that often stays out until 4 a.m. and sleeps until 5 or 6 in the evening.

As we climbed into my car, I asked Omar about his family's reaction to his choice to be a Michael Jackson impersonator. They were most definitely not impressed, he said, but they treated him "normally." Within a month of our interview, he left to spend six months in England in an attempt to make it onto a television program there. His parents helped support him financially with this endeavor.

Omar first started working as a dancer, even though he identifies himself as an "impersonator" on his website and business cards. He has 10,000 cards printed at a time. When I asked, Omar claimed that he is both an impersonator and a tribute artist. "I could have gone to Japan to be a singer and dancer, but I'm just starting to get into singing," he told me.

When Michael Jackson died, Omar received so many text messages on his phone that he thought an alarm was going off. They all said about the same thing: "I'm so sorry to hear about Michael." He finally spoke to a friend who told him that Michael Jackson died of cardiac arrest.

"The first thing I said was, 'What was he arrested for?'"

When Omar's friend then explained that Michael Jackson died from a heart attack, it all made much more sense to him. Omar recalls that he was sad at Michael Jackson's passing, but also saw it as an opportunity to bring his version of Michael Jackson to the rest of the world. He received a little boost when CNN interviewed him after a performance and he auditioned for *So You Think You Can Dance*, a talent-show competition on FOX. He thought he was going to break into the big-time when he made it to the third round, but SONY wouldn't authorize the use of Michael Jackson's music, so he had to drop out of the competition.

As we drove to his show, Omar reflected on his future and his own work. "The remixes and dance mixes I make on YouTube blend Michael Jackson's music with Bollywood music. I can go to the U.K. or to India and release them on the pop charts and perform publicly and on TV because there are no copyright restrictions there. You know, before he died, Michael Jackson was more of a comedy act; I could feel that when I performed for people. But after he died, people took him and his work more seriously. I really think there is a lot of room to grow Michael Jackson's work in new directions."

When we arrived at *Hatam*, I realized that it was in the middle of a typical Southern

Californian strip-mall. We went through the service entrance in back and all the kitchen staff seemed to know Omar and yelling, "Michael Jackson!" as he passed through. He stopped to pose for pictures with the cooks and wait staff, taking a couple of spins between large industrial ovens and stainless-steel prep tables. Then, we took a small elevator to the second floor where he piled his "Billie Jean" outfit and a black shirt with silver brocade on a chair in a storage closet. Someone had informed the DJ of Omar's arrival and suddenly we heard the beginning of one of his "Thriller" remixes. Omar walked to the top of a long, curved staircase leading to the dining area. Below, about sixty, well-dressed Persian women had gathered at long tables. Omar descended the stairwell, dancing his way down the stairs and stopping in front of a tall flagstone waterfall on one side of the room. When the song finished, the restaurant's owner and MC for the night addressed the women in Farsi, encouraging them to express their appreciation. Omar exited and then shortly returned in his black jacket. One of Omar's "Billie Jean" remixes thumped as he commenced with the main body of his act.

Omar is a muscular and athletic 5 foot 10 inches tall, and he jumped through his dance sequences as if performing a gymnastics routine. His movement was abrupt and athletic and fast—almost exaggerated—and lacked the fluidity and lightness of the Michael Jackson's actual dance routines. In performance, it seemed as if he had strung together a number of Michael Jackson's most well known moves, but without a cohesive choreography anchoring it to the particular music video or era. He dropped to the ground on his knees and popped up again—one of his own moves—as the women whooped and hollered and cheered. Then, when he finished, they clapped politely and gathered around for photographs. The women expressed a respectful, subdued appreciation. The audience's reaction exposed something about the show: it was, perhaps, too familiar and somewhat tired to them. When I ask Omar how often he had performed there, he said, "Um, I dunno, close to a hundred times, I guess."

Omar finished around 11 p.m. and suggested that we go to In and Out and he could repay me for gas with dinner. Still attired in his Michael Jackson outfit, including the mirrored sunglasses, Omar attracted a lot of attention in the restaurant's bright dining room. Customers asked him to dance, they asked to take his picture, and he agreed to everything and requested nothing in return.

The altruistic nature of Omar's interactions impressed me. He seemed delighted to be recognized and appreciated for his skills of mimicry. He nonchalantly accepted expressions of praise and affection, for himself, and the appreciation intended for the real

Michael Jackson. This is something that I had observed previously during Sean Vezina's in-character walks around Hollywood Boulevard, and I have heard it repeated in many of the interviews with many other representers. Yes, they may perform, or represent, because they can dance, or sing, like Michael Jackson, or because they bear a resemblance to him, but they also have a great fondness and affection for their subject. They thrive in their immersion in this performance, and they thrive on the attention of an audience that also loves Michael Jackson.

JEN AMERSON

In many ways, Jen Amerson's Michael Jackson represents almost every contradiction and possibility available within the Michael Jacksons community. A white, 37 year-old female impersonator from New Zion, South Carolina, Jen performs at private events, primarily for African-American audiences. Though she has only performed professionally since 2009, during the summer months she can support her two children with the income she earns impersonating Michael Jackson at parties, reunions, and meetings. When we met, before a performance at the Clarion Hotel in Myrtle Beach, she was already in character, dressed in a black sequined jacket with a white sequined armband, black pants with a red stripe down the outside of each leg, and silver sequined socks. The black fedora on her head, tipped just slightly, cast a shadow over her dark aviator sunglasses. Black lines across her cheek and the tip of her nose sharpened her features. She would be the sole entertainment that night at the reunion of a local African-American family in the hotel's ballroom.

Jen performed on a small rectangle of parquet floor in the middle of the ballroom, dancing and lip-synching to "Billie Jean," "Smooth Criminal," "Beat It," and "Dangerous." She appeared self-conscious about her dance moves, but she augmented and loosened up standard impersonators' choreography with personal touches and interpretations, drawing polite applause from the crowd after each song. The children who lined the floor's edge exhibited much more engagement with her performance. They smiled and sang along, reaching out to Jen, who rushed over and grabbed their hands, exuding a genuine warmth and kindness. After performing she posed for photographs and spoke to guests, staying until everyone who wanted a photograph had an opportunity to take his or her souvenir snapshot.

Jen is aware that being a Michael Jackson impersonator is unusual and culturally charged, but for her it really is just a workable, satisfying way to make a living. Jen has been a devoted Michael Jackson fan for as long as she has listened to music. So, when the

DuPont plant where she had worked for more than ten years shut down, and, soon after, she and her husband divorced, Jen turned a loving obsession with Michael Jackson into a good job. And it is clear that her performance is born of affection.

Unlike a couple of the other performers, most notably Jovan, she has not had to fend off criticism or direct harassment related to race, even though, as a single, white mother impersonating an African-American superstar, and as one of only a handful of women performing as Michael Jackson, she is crossing lots of cultural boundaries. "It's definitely a different thing to do in the South," she said. It is, in fact, a different thing to do anywhere, but ultimately it is what the Michael Jacksons are all about—expressing something different within the common character of Michael Jackson and exploring —and expanding—the boundaries of race, class, gender, and ultimately, humanity.

CHARLES JAMES (AKA SCOOBY AND MJ.5)

Charles "Scooby" James grew up in Queens Village; a primarily African-American middle-class neighborhood of wide streets lined by one and two-story homes in Queens, New York. In 2009, Scooby won a talent show at St. John's University, where he was a student, performing a Michael Jackson routine, and this began his public career as a Michael Jackson. When I met him, the range of his circuit was limited to local parties and events in Queens, and sidewalk performances in Times Square. Scooby saw his Michael Jackson work as a temporary station on the road towards a career managing and booking other performers.

When Scooby was a boy in the late 1990s, he saw a Michael Jackson performance and developed a fascination with him. He began emulating Michael Jackson's style of dance and performed around the house for his family. His performance skills developed, and he continued practicing into his teen years. Sometime during high school, his sister said to him, "You know, you can make money doing that." Inspired, he kept working at it—he watched, learned more routines, and practiced for hours upon hours. When Michael Jackson died, on the day Scooby graduated from high school, he felt it marked a spiritual connection between himself and his idol.

After winning the talent show at school Scooby continued working at Applebee's to support himself, pay for school, and help out his parents with their household expenses. When he won an amateur night competition at the Apollo not long after, he became more committed to his Michael Jackson performance career. He took his paycheck, and a refund check from his college financial aid, to buy Michael Jackson costumes on eBay.

It was during his freshman at St. John's University that Scooby began traveling to Manhattan and performing in Times Square. He was inspired to do so when he walked through Times Square one night and saw a man wearing a Spiderman suit with a pouch stuffed with cash at his waist. The Spiderman posed for pictures with people and they paid him for it. Scooby thought it looked like an easy way to make money, and he quickly put together an early version of his Michael Jackson costume. But Scooby drew a strict distinction between himself and his performance persona: he did not wear make-up and he covered his eyes with sunglasses while he performing so that he would not be recognized. His first night on Times Square Scooby made $76, and the second night he made $80. Pleased with this, Scooby invested more money in costumes and learned how apply make-up so he could create his preferred Michael Jackson—the mid-1980s *Thriller* era Michael Jackson.

As Scooby began frequenting Times Square over many months, he recognized that he could make more money when he stood still and posed for pictures with tourists. But still, people asked him to perform. So like any wise businessperson, Scooby adjusted his product, and his fees. He began charging $5 to perform the length of a whole song, and $1 for a spin, a classic move, and a couple of pops. Scooby also discovered that people preferred that he remain in character when he interacted with them, so he affects a soft, high-sounding voice when working. He calls it his "Michael Jackson's voice."

For Scooby, race--and blackness in particular--are so ingrained, and so enforced, in America that they seem almost mundane. They are not nearly as notable as these issues of cultural identity are for Jovan Rameau. When passersby comment about Michael Jackson's racial identity, and about Scooby's identity, the words do not echo for him the way they do for Jovan; they merely reflect a daily fact of life. This is not to say that Scooby is impervious to the institutional racism under which he struggles.

Unlike Jovan, Scooby has a less reliable schedule for his paid presentations. He performs some weekends—more often when a holiday falls on a weekend day and he can get away from school—but he mainly works in Times Square on warm weekend nights. He reports that he experiences racially charged episodes in New York City during his 7 p.m. to midnight shifts near Broadway. When he first started performing in Times Square, he brought a friend to manage the music on the boom box—and to guard it from thieves while he performed. On the third night he was there, two police officers approached him and told him he needed a permit in order to perform with music on a public sidewalk. Scooby wasn't pleased, but he quit for the night. Unhappy with the event, Scooby did some research and discovered that individuals can perform on New York City sidewalks without a permit as long as they do not play music through a loud speaker. The next time he performed, Scooby wore his iPod and earphones to help time his dance routine. People gathered, he danced and posed with them, he even made a little bit of money, but again the police confronted him.

"You need to leave the sidewalk," they told him.

"But I'm not doing anything wrong," Scooby retorted.

The police insisted, as he was causing a "commotion," claiming that the size of the crowd of he drew was too large. Though he disagreed, Scooby left the area, moving up the block to another part of the sidewalk. Scooby reports that this is a continuing problem and the altercations with the police in Times Square are ongoing. While he had no hard proof, he suspected that the police response to his activities were racially motivated. Scooby reported that he had seen a white performer—albeit not a Michael Jackson representer—in the same location on the sidewalk, with a similar sized audience, and that person was *not* told to leave. Scooby has noticed, too, that when the police tell him he is not allowed to work in a certain space because people cannot pass easily on the sidewalk, the police often stay after he leaves. Scooby says he has then seen tourists stop and talk with police and ask to take pictures with them, attracting a similar-sized group of people. The police never seem in a hurry to disband these gatherings, according to Scooby.

Scooby, like Jovan, is very clear about his perception of Michael Jackson's race. When I asked him if he sees Michael Jackson as "black," he says yes without hesitation. Furthermore, Scooby doesn't think Michael Jackson abandoned his culture—his black identity—as others maintain. When he performs in an open public setting like Times Square, people will occasionally comment about his skin color—naturally deep brown with reddish undertones—and compare it to Jackson's. He told me that the only consistent comment he hears is the ironic, "I thought Michael Jackson was white" line. Notably, Scooby says that he does not experience the quantity or range of comments that Jovan reports from Hollywood Boulevard, even though his audience, like Jovan's, is racially mixed and culturally diverse.

At the time of this interview with Scooby, he was in his third year at the state university in Hicksville, New York, where he studied entertainment management. He had taken an afternoon train from school to perform his version of Michael Jackson at a nine-year-old's birthday party. The child's mother was a friend of Scooby's sister. It was October 2011, and my train was delayed so that I arrived two hours late to meet Scooby at his house in Queens.

Scooby's sister and her husband drove us to Nora's house, where Nora was hosting the party for her son Unique. Scooby removed his backpack and a suitcase full of costumes and make-up from the car and entered the house. I followed. His performance as Michael Jackson was intended to be a surprise. Nora introduced us to the adults in the front room, describing Scooby as the "talent" for the night, and me as "his photographer." The party guests began guessing what Scooby could be performing while Unique and six of his friends played in an adjacent room. Nora seemed ecstatic to have Scooby there, and assured us that everyone would love the surprise. A general cacophony enveloped the house as the children screamed and played, the television blared, a radio played and a DJ began spinning out in the backyard.

Nora showed Scooby and me to an upstairs bedroom where he put his bags. Nora told Scooby he could change and apply his make-up there. Downstairs in the kitchen Nora's friends prepared mountains of hot dogs, collard greens, potatoes, and hamburgers for the party guests. Just before leaving to pick up Unique's birthday cake, Nora whispered to Scooby that she would like him to perform "Rock with You," a Michael Jackson song from the late 1970s album *Off the Wall*. Scooby looked a little confused. He had not practiced the number and he confessed to me that did not know the words, let alone have a copy of it to practice with before he would go on.

His performance was scheduled to start at 6 p.m., just after the sun set and it would be dark enough to see the lights in the stage area, inside the two-car garage behind the house. We decided it was best to hide out in Nora's room, and wait the two hours until his performance. Scooby fell asleep on Nora's bed. I sat beside him listening to the party below. Scooby told me that on weekend nights, to earn extra money, he sells Nutcrackers, a drink he concocted from juices mixed with alcohol. He bottles it in his room at the fraternity house, and sells it at parties around campus. From an $80 investment he could make $200 a night, which was more than he would make in a week at Applebee's. At Unique's party he would make $175, a discounted rate from the regular fee of $350 because Nora is a friend of the family. Scooby planned to buy a new car--his previous car was towed and he couldn't afford to pay the tickets and fines to retrieve it. Scooby also planned buy more, and better, Michael Jackson clothes, which he believed would help to raise his profile in the Michael Jacksons community so he could land more, and better, gigs.

At around 5:15 p.m., Scooby opened his suitcase and pulled out a Styrofoam wig stand, a red faux-leather jacket, and a black sequined top. Downstairs, irregular screams and hollers pierced the floor as the birthday boy and his friends played. A small white bucket and dirty cardboard sign with black lettering that read "Tips Appreciated" fell to the floor. Scooby explained that he uses these when he performs in Times Square. He plugged in his iPod and music played from its very small speakers as he tried to get into character. He opened a shoebox full of props—make-up, the sparkly white glove, extra rhinestones, and glue. He then began the long process of transformation.

When Scooby committed to performing Michael Jackson in public, the first item he bought was a red sequined jacket. Then he bought a black sequined jacket similar to what Michael Jackson wore in the "Billie Jean" music video, and finally he bought a version of the red "Thriller" jacket. The first outfit that he wore to the talent show displays his ingenuity and attention to detail—it included the red jacket and black pants with electrical tape running down the outer seam of each leg. He also created armbands from the electrical tape. Scooby also sewed rubber bands in the cuffs to fit them properly. He made his first white glove from a golf glove with black streaks between the fingers, onto which he glued individual rhinestones. Since he wore no make-up then, his preparation time was very short.

Since those early days, Scooby's transformation has become more elaborate and involved. In Nora's room, he first applied foundation to his entire face. The foundation, called "Honey Glow," is the lightest shade that Scooby could buy. He put a glob of it on a small white sponge and wiped it on his entire face, starting with his left cheek. Once he covered his face from hairline to shirt collar, he applied powder with a small brush. The brush was falling apart, and he stopped every once in a while to pull hairs off of the surface of his face. Michael Jackson representers all seem to pay close attention to creating the illusion of his nose. Some spend the majority of their preparation time applying light and dark powder to his small, bobbed-tipped nose, while others just let their own nose stand and add black eyeliner around their nostrils to disguise the shape. Scooby's nose is much wider and flatter than Michael Jackson's nose was after the plastic surgeries of the mid-to-late-1980s. Scooby applied another shade of foundation—simply called "Beige"— along the bridge to tip and from side to side. The idea he said is to "make it pop" from the rest of his face. He penciled black eyeliner to create shadowing along the sides and the underside of his nose. He told me he used so much eyeliner that it was the one make-up item he spent the most money on.

Scooby then filled in his eyebrows with the eyeliner, shaping them into sharp, upside-down V-shapes, capturing one of Michael Jackson's most distinguishing features. He also used the eyeliner to form circles under his cheekbones, supporting the illusion that his face was thinner and more angular. Scooby added a small amount down the middle of his chin to create the cleft chin. He draws in a modified hairline on his forehead and on the sides of his face, using the tip of a mascara brush, wielding it confidently and making no mistakes, so that one side parallels the other as he forms the curvature. Before Scooby studied entertainment management he studied graphic design, and these days he also designs t-shirts. "I am very good at drawing," he says, indicating that his design skills help with his make-up regimen.

With the make-up complete, he removed the wig from its stand and repositioned the bobby pins to hold down little unruly hairs. This wig was very full and did not have the tendrils in the front that characterized Michael Jackson's hair, but it didn't seem to matter to Scooby. Scooby then pulled on a pair of white socks covered with small plastic-metallic, sequin-like circles, a less expensive version than what Michael Jackson actually wore. He pulled on his black pants with a black satin stripe down each leg. Then he looked for his red leather jacket. It was not real leather, he informed me; he got it for $20 on eBay earlier in the year. He would wear simple black loafers, worn at the soles and toes from heavy use on the pavement in Times Square. He then looked around for the last piece of his costume— the bejeweled glove. Many of the rhinestones had fallen off. "If I had time, I'd glue the extra ones on where there are holes," he said. He seemed a little embarrassed about this aspect of his costume, but he pulled the glove onto his left hand and pushed the sleeves of his red jacket to just under his elbows.

It was almost time to go downstairs when a knock at the door, interrupted us and Nora let herself in. "They're ready for you, Michael!" she said. She appeared very excited and impressed by the quality of Scooby's appearance. Scooby handed me a CD of the music he needed for his performance and asked me to give it to the DJ, indicating which track to start with. Nora then led me downstairs, through the house, and out the backdoor.

"It's almost time!!!" she shouted to the guests assembled in her backyard.

The kids played a guessing game: "Who is it?" one asked.

"Justin Timberlake!"

"Justin Beiber!"

"Usher!"

The small backyard brimmed with guests—adults and children—standing on the stairs, sitting on the fence, and seated in chairs lined up against the fence. A DJ spun records from a booth in a corner. He had arranged a stack of colored lights pointed towards the garage directly behind the house. The garage door gaped open and small white lights were strung along the inside of the doorframe. A large silver garland hung low across the front of the garage and a mirrored ball spun front and center, perfectly placed to capture and reflect the light. Partygoers inside the garage pulled apart another strand of garland and threw the pieces across the floor. The collective effort meant to emulate a nightclub dance floor.

Suddenly screams pierced the night and the crowd hushed a bit as the DJ music lulled. Scooby appeared. Grown women, then children, rushed towards him, almost knocking him over. Scooby marched his way through the crowd of more than twenty people until he reached center stage, below the mirror ball. Two women in particular—especially Nora—screamed wildly, "MICHAEL!! MICHAEL!!" They shouted, falling over each other as Scooby walked by. As the first few notes of "Beat It" thumped, Scooby raised a prop microphone to his mouth and began lip synching the first line, "They told him don't you ever come around here. . ." Nora and her friend dissolved into fits of joy, screaming, "Michael!," and falling into each other's arms.

Scooby performed to a mash-up of Michael Jackson's music that he created specifically for his performances. In performance, Scooby weaves thirty-second segments of songs into a montage of Michael Jackson's greatest hits. "Beat It," fades into the sounds of a cheering crowd which leads into "Billie Jean." This format repeats—song segment to crowd noise to song. "Beat It" to "Billie Jean" to "Bad" to "Smooth Criminal."

Scooby's goal is to "create the illusion that he is still here." At the end of this abbreviated set, some of the audience rushed him. They wanted to be photographed with Scooby in his Michael Jackson persona, to dance next to him, and with him—they wanted to dance with each other and sing Michael Jackson songs together. The energy his presence inspired and transcended the size and scale of that backyard in Queens.

After the initial performance, the audience began wandering off, some going back inside the house, some milling about in the yard. It was dark and growing cold. Eventually, Scooby also went inside to refresh and change his costume in anticipation of performing "Rock with You," as requested by Nora. Upstairs, Scooby draped himself in his black sequined jacket—the Billie Jean jacket. Nora asked Scooby to accompany Unique while he cut the birthday cake.

"Yes, sure," he replied in his soft lilting voice Michael Jackson voice.

While mixing among the party guests Scooby tried to remain in his character though he was unable to maintain the performance throughout the night. As everyone gathered around for the cake cutting, it became clear that Unique was not terribly comfortable with being the center of such attention *and* with having "Michael Jackson" there. Unique squirmed a bit and shied away from Scooby while everyone sang "Happy Birthday."

Scooby sang in his natural voice. During these interactions it became clear that Scooby's presence, and his performance was really intended to please the adult friends and family, not necessarily Unique.

After the cake was cut and the pieces were passed around on paper plates, Scooby went back upstairs to Nora's room to find the lyrics to "Rock With You." He had very little time to learn the song and prepare its presentation in his mind. While Nora went to discuss things with the DJ, the kids returned to playing with tops on the floor. People began saying good-bye to Nora and the party generally seemed to be ending.

Suddenly, Scooby returned, walking through the house to the backyard. Nora and her friend screamed and yelled all the way through the house following him out the back door. He picked up his microphone as music started and Nora and her friend continued screaming. In the midst of this, Nora's friend appeared to swoon and fell to the ground. Although she was visibly pregnant, no one seemed concerned about her fall. Scooby swayed and lip-synced to the music, occasionally turning and spinning. The kids were nowhere to be found, only the adults remained for this performance. The bank of colored lights and the fog machine Nora rented ran at full bore and bands of colored light seemed to radiate from Scooby. While he sang and swayed through "Rock with You," the remaining audience held each other and sang along with him. It seemed new and exciting and nostalgic, and perhaps somewhat contrived. I got the impression that the women there, like Nora and her friend believe that Michael Jackson was really present, at least for brief moments. They wanted to be near him, touch him, and hug him. They wanted to take part in this ritual, as Scooby represented something greater than himself, something greater than themselves, something perhaps transcendent. However, even as they screamed and swooned and called out to Michael Jackson, it had become difficult to know if this was authentic behavior—an actual emotional reaction—or if it was an act performed for each other, or for Scooby, to help validate the experience. In the end, it might not matter how "authentic" the behavior was to begin with, since the function of release through emotional and physical exhaustion was achieved. The entire event seemed like certain religious rites where ecstatic outpourings are an objective achieved by summoning the presence of the holy spirit, or some avatar of the divine. In this context, in a backyard in Queens, New York, that avatar was Michael Jackson as enacted by Scooby.

CONCLUSION

he fifth anniversary of Michael Jackson's death is just a few short
months away, and it is true that, even now, the question of exactly
who Michael Jackson was remains ambiguous, if not unanswerable.
The raw facts of his life, an African-American boy who struggled
against great odds—institutionalized racism, poverty, an overbearing
and abusive father—who, through sheer talent and grit, raised himself
to a position as one the world's wealthiest and most identifiable and iconic figures, is the
stuff of legends. His is a true story, and Michael Jackson was a living human being, however
extraordinary; but nothing about Michael Jackson's life was ordinary, easy, or simple.
The history of the culture from which he emerged, the musical and performance traditions
he absorbed, and the place he carved out for himself, defy pithy explanations and straight
analysis. What can be said is that as a man he was as flawed as any other, as a performer
he was without peer, and as an icon he—as an ideal—Michael Jackson lives on. Michael
Jackson's music and performances and image have become fully entrenched in worldwide
popular culture, even as his personal foibles recede into irrelevance.

What remains is Michael Jackson's work and, for many, that ideal. Michael Jackson's
work as a performer flowed from the cross currents of African-American and mainstream
American culture. His art displayed both a deliberate, conscious selection from these
sources and an enormous well of unconscious influence that shaped him and drove him,
and which informed his work. Michael Jackson described himself as a black man, but in
the way he created himself, and his image, he de-essentialized what it meant to be black.
Indeed, he also de-essentialized what it meant to be a father, to be an adult, and to be

male. In doing so, he inadvertently communicated that these categories are not 'real,' but are instead socio-historical constructs.[1] To paraphrase the poet T.S Eliot, he could not say *just* what he meant—and everything he said, and did, expressed *more* than he intended—perhaps. Which is not say that Michael Jackson was not deliberate in the messages and meanings he expressed through his music and dance, the characters he played in his performances and videos, and the public persona he recreated again and again.

But conscious intentions and subconscious expressions struggle within the psyches of all people, and especially within the psyches of great artists. Certainly Michael Jackson could not control how his work—and his identity—would be received and interpreted by others, or how they might intellectually and emotionally integrate his messages and work, or how they would eventually reinterpret this; this is the work of the Michael Jackson representers. This is the play space where they assume Michael Jackson's symbols and signifiers and rework them to suit their own idea of what Michael Jackson is, and where their own conscious and unconscious choices, and their own talents and limitations, forge new and endless variations of Michael Jackson. As much as Michael Jackson himself, this has been the subject of this study.

The representers I have known, in all of their glorious inconsistencies and commonalities, challenge what it means to be a Michael Jackson impersonator and who may be considered a Michael Jackson performer, and how Michael Jackson can be validly presented. Like Michael Jackson's own life, this challenges many of our personal and cultural notions of social roles, race, gender, and sexuality. These performers are widely diverse in their origins, and the means they employ to interpret Michael Jackson are wildly different and endlessly ingenious. Some have developed sewing talents and clothing design skills that would be admired in any New York fashion house. Some simply imply the image of Michael Jackson with a found and shabby fedora or a single sparkly glove. Some adorn themselves in high-quality specialty costumes from across the globe. The costume (or mere costume element, as in the hat or glove)—the sign—is important, but not so much the quality. Identification begins with the readily available symbol—the sign of identification with Michael Jackson—and all else, including race, gender, class, and sexuality, is mere detail.

I have been intrigued by these performers' free use of stagecraft, make-up, and costume, and by their ritualistic transformation into the Michael Jackson they want to be. Mirroring Michael Jackson's own physical transformations, a representer often takes great pains to emulate his facial features from whatever era they choose to present.

But their make-up often also draws attention to *itself* as much as it transforms and disguises the performer—as much as it blends their face with the image of Michael Jackson. The representers bring attention to the artifice of this play even as they strive for authenticity, which complicates and enriches the experience. And all bring attention to themselves, informing the world with these gestures and symbols that they represent Michael Jackson.

Ultimately, the representer's medium is his or her body; their bodies are the canvas upon which they paint their portrait of Michael Jackson. Through craft and physical skill, representers reshape, contort, paint, and decorate their bodies into a new physical manifestation and *then* begin the actual physical work of performance. The body is a site for communicating these points with their audience, confirming the representer's related identity choices—the name they self-apply, the appearance they present, and the interpretation of race they enact in their representation of Michael Jackson.

In field observation, and in the photo studio with lookalikes, impersonators, and tribute artists, I often witnessed how easily they step in and out of their various roles. They shift between their performance of the Michael Jackson character and their own persona, acting nearly simultaneously as object and subject. Different performers slide between personas and identities in differing degrees. In the photo studio, Devra and Omar performed Michael Jackson in front of the camera, then turned the performance off to be themselves once the camera was away. Both Sean and Jovan perform Michael Jackson in highly public places but then communicate with their audience as themselves while still in costume. Scooby tries to create a more all-encompassing performance, filling in the spaces between dance routines by speaking and acting his interpretation of Michael Jackson, though he is not able to sustain this continually.

Why does this happen? How can the representers *be* Michael Jackson the entertainer one moment, and then seamlessly *be* themselves at another, even while still costumed? The impact of these shifts between personas is uncanny, if not disconcerting. It seems that Michael Jackson is to them not so much a real person, but a character that can be customized by grafting their own interpretation of dress, of dance, of name, and even of race, onto his foundation. The result is a completely unique entity, even while it refers to the original, acting as a place of worship and nostalgia and a point of exchange between the representers and the audience.

That people create definitions for themselves through their own experiences is not a new concept. That popular American culture is a powerful force that can suggest, and enforce, identity through the construction and deconstruction of racial and gender and generational barriers is also not a groundbreaking notion. That the represenrs choose to actively engage these forces and contradictions and ambiguities, and play with these images of race, gender, fatherhood, adulthood, and even sexuality, through the play of their Michael Jackson presentations *is* new. Theirs is a compelling response to essentialism— and proscribed racial, gender, and generational roles—that helps us understand emerging questions about contemporary, evolving social identities.

If Michael Jackson were not such a towering image, if his talent had not been so enormous, and if his drive toward self-determination had not been so fierce, the possibilities expressed by the performers I have studied and presented might lay dormant. But even now, nearly five years after his untimely death, Michael Jackson continues exerting enormous influence in our culture. Through the work of the Michael Jacksons, this influence appears to grow and expand in meaning and the potential to liberate our notions of identity and self-expression.

ENDNOTES

INTRODUCTION
June 2009, Memorials on the Street, Harlem, New York City

i CNN. *"Jackson fans pack Harlem for Apollo memorial."* http://www.cnn.com/2009/SHOWBIZ/Music/06/30/jackson.apollo.html (Accessed on July 19, 2013.)

ii Greg Tate, "Michael Jackson: The Man in Our Mirror," *Village Voice*, July 1, 2009, accessed July 11, 2013, http://www.villagevoice.com/2009-07-01/news/michael-jackson-the-man-in-our-mirror.html.

iii Greg Tate, "Michael Jackson: The Man in Our Mirror."

CHAPTER ONE
"The pure products of America/go crazy." A Career Overview

1 Nelson George, *Where Did Our Love Go?: The Rise and Fall of the Motown Sound* (Urbana: University of Illinois Press, 2007), 184.

2 "Michael Jackson", *Rolling Stone*, http://www.rollingstone.com/music/artists/michael-jackson.html. Adapted from "Triumph & Tragedy: The Life of Michael Jackson", August 25, 2009. Accessed on January 27, 2014.

3 Martin Luther King Jr., "Beyond Vietnam" (speech, New York City, April 4, 1967), Fact Monster, http://www.factmonster.com/spot/mlkspeeches.html .

4 Soul Tracks. "Vanity Fair celebrates an oral history of Motown." Accessed January 31, 2014. http://www.soultracks.com/story-motown_vanity.

5 Zimbio. "Music History Berry Gordy: I hired a white salesman for the South. I didn't have pictures of black artists on the record covers." Accessed January 31, 2014. http://www.zimbio.com/Barry+Gordy/articles/GSZxG0ylXf0/Music+History+Berry+Gordy+hired+white+salesman.

6 Soulful Detroit. "Vanity Fair: Motown the Untold Stories. The Label's Greatest Legends in Their Own Words." (Full article, "It Happened in Hitsville", by Lisa Robinson, December 2008 available.) Accessed January 31, 2014. http://soulfuldetroit.com/showthread.php?8617-Vanity-Fair-Motown-The-Untold-Stories-The-Labels-Greatest-Legends-in-their-own-words&s=cd0c794ecbdcccbe1f27fa4f6adff451.

7 Rollo Romig, "Dancing in The Street: Detroit's Radical Anthem," *New Yorker*, July 22, 2013, accessed July 1, 2013, http://www.newyorker.com/online/blogs/books/2013/07/dancing-in-the-street-detroits-radical-anthem.html.

8 The Root. "Movement Music: How Motown became the country's soundtrack for change." Accessed January 31, 2014. http://www.theroot.com/articles/culture/2009/01/motown_at_50.html.

9 Jason King, "Michael Jackson: An Appreciation of His Talent," in *Best Music Writing 2010*, eds. Ann

Powers and Daphne Carr (Cambridge: Da Capo Press, 2010) http://passthecurve.com/post/28925432757/michaeljacksonanappreciation.html.

[10] Mathew Delmont, "Michael Jackson & Television Before Thriller," *The Journal of Pan African Studies, 3:7* (2010): 101-119.

[11] Michael Jackson, *Moonwalk* (New York: Random House, 1988), 87-8.

[12] BBC. *"The Culture Show."* http://www.youtube.com/watch?v=iZqD_VWBGDE.html. (Accessed on July 5, 2013).

[13] Michael Jackson, *Moonwalk*, 101.

[14] John Rockwell, "Michael Jackson's Thriller: Superb Job," *The New York Times*, December 19, 1982, accessed on June 15, 2013, http://www.nytimes.com/1982/12/19/arts/michael-jackson-s-thriller-superb-job.html

[15] Michael Jackson, *Moonwalk*, 52.

[16] Michael Eric Dyson, "Michael Jackson's Postmodern Spirituality", in *The Michael Eric Dyson Reader* (New York: Basic Civitas Books, 2004), 37.

[17] BBC. *"The Culture Show."* http://www.youtube.com/watch?v=iZqD_VWBGDE.html. (Accessed on July 5, 2013).

[18] Jay Cocks, "Why He's a Thriller," *TIME*, March 19, 1984, accessed July 30, 2013, http://content.time.com/time/magazine/article/0,9171,950053,00.html.

[19] Dyson, *Michael Jackson's Postmodern Spirituality*, 444.

[20] J. Edward Keyes, "Michael Jackson's Indelible Pop Legacy," *Rolling Stone*, July 7, 2009, accessed on June 7, 2013, http://www.rollingstone.com/music/news/michael-jacksons-indelible-pop-legacy-20090707.html.

[21] "Michael Jackson", *Rolling Stone*.

[22] PrimeTime Live. *"Prime-Time Live Interview With Michael Jackson & Lisa Marie Presley."* (Part 2/6) http://www.youtube.com/watch?v=KMwHfeG2IEI. (Accessed on February 18, 2012)

CHAPTER TWO
"The all-American fascination with Blackness." The Performance of Race, A Brief History

[1] Greg Tate, "Nigs R Us Or How Blackfolk Became Fetish Objects," in *Everything But the Burden*, ed. Greg TateNew York: Random House, 2003) http://www.randomhouse.com/boldtype/0303/tate/excerpt.html.

[2] W.T. Lhamon, *Raising Cain: Blackface Performance from Jim Crow to Hip Hop* (Cambridge: Harvard University Press, 1998), 97.

³ Eric Lott, *Love & Theft: Blackface Minstrelsy and the American Working Class* (New York: Oxford University Press), 26.

⁴ Louis Chude-Sokei, *The Last "Darky": Bert Williams, Black-On-Black Minstrelsy, and the African Diaspora*, (Durham: Duke University Press, 2006), 2.

⁵ J. Martin Favor *Authentic Blackness: The Folk in the New Negro Renaissance* (Durham: Duke University Press, 1993), 123.

⁶ Michael Eric Dyson, "Michael Jackson's Postmodern Spirituality", in *The Michael Eric Dyson Reader* (New York: Basic Civitas Books, 2004), 37.

⁷ Dyson, *Michael Jackson's Postmodern Spirituality*, 444.

⁸ Sylvia Martin. "The Roots and Routes of Michael Jackson's Global Identity," *Social Science and Modern Society*, no. 49 (2011): 285–286.

⁹ BBC."*The Culture Show*." http://www.youtube.com/watch?v=iZqD_VWBGDE.html. (Accessed on July 5, 2013).

CHAPTER FIVE
"Katherine Jackson was in tears when she saw him." **How Representers Construct Their Michael Jackson**

¹ This aspect of classification translates to world of professional mimicry, but for this analysis, I will speak specifically about those who represent Michael Jackson.

² Lois McElravy and Steve Weber, "A Couple of Characters", Speaker Magazine, vol. 6/5 (January/February 2012), 18-21.

CHAPTER SIX
"How do I look right now? Do I look like Michael Jackson?" **Narratives of Representers**

¹ "The light-skinned Michael", is another performer who is Caucasian who performs on the Walk of Fame on Hollywood Boulevard too. I've never met the person Jovan refers to here.

² Jovan was not able to provide the name of the psychologist who told him this. The quote comes from the book's website which is a list of many of the comments Jovan has collected.

CONCLUSION

¹ Willa Stillwater, PhD and Joie Collins, Dancing With the Elephant: Conversations about Michael Jackson, his art, and social change. Accessed on November 24, 2011, May 10, 2012. http://dancingwith-theelephant.wordpress.com/2012/03/08/roundtable-the-mj-academia/.

The Michael Jacksons
Copyright © Lorena H. Turner 2014

Photo editor: Meg Handler
Editors: Joanna Lehan and Jean Dykstra

First Edition / Spring 2014
ISBN 978-1-62890-955-5
Printed in China

Little Moth Press
4906 Glenalbyn Drive
Los Angeles, California 90065

Printed and bound by C + C Offset Printing Co., Ltd.

BOOK DESIGN BY FRANCESCA RICHER, NYC